OLIVER CROMWELL
*(from the painting by Robert Walker in the
National Portrait Gallery, London)*

OLIVER CROMWELL
by C. V. WEDGWOOD

Great Lives

DUCKWORTH
3 HENRIETTA STREET
LONDON   W.C.2

First published 1939
Reprinted 1941, 1947, 1956, 1962

Printed in Great Britain
by Gilmour & Dean Ltd., Glasgow and London

FOR
ALICE PAWSON

CONTENTS

7

in the Army – unsuccessful attempts at mediation –
the Army seizes the King – and marches on London
– Cromwell's negotiations with the King – and
with the Army officers – flight of the King – Crom-
well's opinion hardens against Charles – Second
Civil War – siege of Pembroke – Battle of Preston –
Pride's Purge – trial and execution of the King –
Cromwell's motives and justification.

House of Lords abolished – mutiny of the Levellers
– the first Irish campaign – the second Irish cam-
paign – the first Scottish campaign – Battle of
Dunbar – the second Scottish campaign – Battle of
Worcester – the Dutch War – tension between
Army and Parliament again – political ideas of
Cromwell and Vane contrasted – Cromwell expels
Parliament – the Little Parliament – resignation of
the Little Parliament.

The Instrument of Government – nature and extent of
Cromwell's power – his Court and family – settlement of Scotland – settlement of Ireland – Cromwell's influence on religion – on education – on the
arts and sciences – legal and administrative reforms
– treaties with lesser Powers – First Protectorate
Parliament – Royalist revolt – the Major-generals –
opposition to Cromwell.

Cromwell's outlook – plans for a Protestant league –
the Vaudois – rivalry of Denmark and Sweden –
Blake in the Mediterranean – breach with Spain –
Santo Domingo and Jamaica – alliance with France
– Santa Cruz – Battle of the Dunes – cession of
Dunkirk – appreciation of Cromwell's policy.

Financial difficulties – Cromwell opens the Second
Protectorate Parliament – *The Humble Petition and
Advice* – Second Session of Parliament – Cromwell
and religion – Cromwell and the administration –
family affairs – death of Lady Claypole – Cromwell's illness and death – his family – his political
beliefs – his achievement.

INTRODUCTION

CROMWELL'S CHARACTER AND SIGNIFICANCE

SAMUEL RAWSON GARDINER, the greatest English historian of the seventeenth century, described Cromwell as " the most typical Englishman of all time." He is to politics what Shakespeare is to literature, the dominant figure to whom our thoughts naturally recur. " He stands there, not to be implicitly followed as a model, but to hold up a mirror to ourselves, wherein we may see alike our weakness and our strength." Nearly half a century has passed since Gardiner wrote those words. New facts have come to light, new angles have been exploited, new interpretations put forward : the history of the past is not static, but alters its face as the present alters. Yet in substance Gardiner's verdict still stands. The essential interest of Cromwell lies in his resemblance to the average man, only with a greater grandeur, so that to read his political struggles is to see the ordinary life magnified and ennobled.

The modern dictator owes his power, in part at least, to the sense among his people that he is an apotheosis of each one of them. This element is inevitably present in all those characters of history who still exercise a fascination over the modern mind. The similarity between all men, dead or living, who have acquired exceptional ascendancy over their fellows, has led to a recent and false over-emphasis on Cromwell as a dictator. He was never wholly autocratic even by the standards of his own time, and he cannot be compared to the modern dictator, the product of economic, social and physical conditions inconceivable in the seventeenth century. Yet in England there has been no ruler so absolute since his time, and the story of his brief domination may have some modern relevance in illuminating the type of man whom this country was once willing to accept as a quasi-absolute ruler.

Cromwell's career illustrates the irreconcilable contradiction between ethics and politics, between the right and the expedient, which is the eternal problem of the statesman. He rose to power on the disintegration of a country under the pressure of civil war. In that war he had himself fought for principles which were to be directly contravened by the establishment of his own rule. But he accepted a position difficult in itself and open to misrepresentation because, in the immediate present, he saw no other way. He who had drawn the sword to save England from her enemies, kept it drawn to save her from her friends.

He was consumed by an intense, narrow, burning patriotism, so closely interwoven with his religion that he could not distinguish one from the other. Both contributed to an over-powering moral self-confidence. This combination of religion, patriotism and personal confidence, not uncommon among the English, makes Cromwell particularly interesting to a generation of his countrymen who may be faced again with his problems, but on a larger scale. His struggle to combine morality with expediency, and the desirable with the possible, makes him an example and a warning to the politicians of all time. In the intermittent recognition of his own failure, in the deliberate and self-imposed blindness to that failure which alone gave him strength to go on, lies his personal tragedy.

CHAPTER I

" IN the year of Our Lord 1599, Oliver, the son
of Robert Cromwell, gentleman, and of Elizabeth
his wife, born on the 25th day of April and bap-
tised on the 29th of the same month." With this
formula, in a simplified Latin, the Register Book
of the Church of St. John the Baptist at Huntingdon records the birth of the Great Protector.

Oliver Cromwell was four generations removed
from a Putney brewer of Welsh origin named
Morgan Williams, who had married Katherine,
elder sister of Thomas Cromwell. Their son,
Richard, who sycophantically adopted the sur-
name of his powerful uncle, acquired considerable
property in East Anglia through the plunder of
the monasteries. Richard's son and Oliver's
grandfather, Sir Henry Cromwell of Hinchinbrook, and the head of the family in 1599, was
commonly known as the " Golden Knight," and
reckoned among the richest men in the district.
The bulk of Sir Henry's estates would pass in
time to his eldest son. Robert, one of the younger
children, had been established in independent
possession of a small property at Huntingdon. He
had married a widow, Elizabeth Lynn, daughter
of Sir William Steward, farmer of the tithes of
Ely Cathedral, a solid and sensible woman of a

Norfolk family which claimed an improbable connection with the Stuart Kings.

Cromwell was thus, like most Englishmen of the upper class, of very mixed ancestry – Welsh, Norman and Anglo-Saxon. Yet, at a superficial view, it would seem that the Norman and Welsh blood were submerged by the Anglo-Saxon. Large and thick-set in body, slow in decision, obstinate in determination, he seemed to belong wholly to East Anglia, to that heavy soil on which he was born, to that flat horizon and those pale skies within whose wide arch he grew up. The analysis of racial characteristics is often misleading, but in examining the deeper recesses of Cromwell's character certain contradictory elements come to light – a fanaticism, a vision, a hidden fire, blazing out suddenly to consume all obstacles and all opponents. These and perhaps certain other less admirable qualities of the Welshman are to be found in him.

Nothing survives from Cromwell's childhood, save a few isolated facts, some doubtful legend and much spiteful gossip. As soon as he was old enough, he was sent to the Free School attached to the Hospital of St. John at Huntingdon. The headmaster, Doctor Thomas Beard, was a ferocious Puritan who believed that the Pope was Anti-Christ, and had translated from the French, in a work entitled *The Theatre of God's Judgements*, a stupendous collection of miraculous punishments summarily inflicted by the Almighty on transgressors. He imbued his pupils with faith in, and fear of, a God who neither overlooked nor forgave the shortcomings of his unhappy creation. In this faith Cromwell was to live and die. But as a schoolmaster Doctor Beard did not apparently emulate the vindictive conduct which he admired in Jehovah ; the affection and respect which he inspired in Cromwell indicate that, although he may have been stern, he was not unsympathetic.

In his seventeenth year Cromwell was removed from school, and on April 23rd, 1616, entered at Sidney Sussex College, Cambridge. The Master at this time was the introspective and meticulous Doctor Samuel Ward, under whom the college was fast becoming a nursery for Puritan doctrine. Cromwell himself was placed under the care of a mild little man not very much older than himself, the Reverend Richard Howlett.

At this period legend – which embellishes the sober history of Cromwell's childhood with such tales as that a monkey stole him from his cradle, that he dreamed he was to be King, that he knocked down the infant Charles I in play – becomes vociferous once again. At Cambridge, so Cromwell's enemies later declared, he had passed his time drinking, whoring, playing football and utterly neglecting his studies. Cromwell himself thickened the fog which obscures this early part of his life by dismissing all his youth in the one sentence : " I lived in and loved darkness and hated the light : I was a chief, the chief, of sinners." To judge by parallel statements made by religious converts, these dreadful words probably mean very little. At Cambridge he doubtless worked as little and amused himself as much as the young men of his time, which is to say that he worked more and played less than the average undergraduate of to-day. He was a normal young man, clumsily but vigorously built, with a keen taste for outdoor sports, for hawking, hunting and games, which he never outgrew. Tales of his early debaucheries remain to this day unsubstantiated, and in the absence of all evidence

Bc

it may be safely assumed that in his youth he was neither monster nor saint. His gifts were certainly not academic and in after life neither his letters nor his speeches show great power of sustained mental concentration. But he knew his classics well and conversed fluently in Latin with the ambassadors of foreign powers, which is evidence enough that he cannot wholly have neglected his books.

He left Cambridge without a degree, little more than a year after his first coming, for no other reason than the sudden death of his father. A legal quibble made it for a time doubtful whether he would not become a royal ward, but the case went at last in favour of his independence, and he found himself at eighteen the master of a small property and responsible for the care of his mother and several unmarried sisters.

Whether in these circumstances Cromwell had the leisure or resources to study law is doubtful. Tradition assigns him to Lincoln's Inn, although most of his kinsmen and friends were at Gray's. The registers of these Inns, as also of the Inner and Middle Temple, know nothing of him. He was, however, in London for some time during his twentieth and twenty-first years, for he had an introduction to a wealthy leather-merchant, Sir James Bourchier, whom he visited at his London house on Tower Hill and at his country house in Essex. Sir James' five sons were still children, and it was not their company, but that of their elder sister, the homely and placid Elizabeth, which Cromwell sought. The marriage was not so brilliant on either side as to preclude the possibility of a love-match. Cromwell's approach to individuals was always impulsive and sincere ; he may have found in the company of this dull and tranquil young woman the peace for which his soul hungered in vain. She herself was twenty-three and single, a sufficient inducement, at a time when marriage was essential to independence and self-respect, to predispose her favourably towards a lover who had as little to offer her in personal attractions as she had to give him. The wedding took place at St. Giles' Cripplegate on August 22nd, 1620.

After his marriage Cromwell returned to Huntingdon to take up his duties as a landowner and farmer. The resources of his household at this time do not seem to have been more than about £300 a year, an income which even in those times was no more than sufficient to the needs of his position as a householder and a gentleman. His lands were wheat-growing, and the low prices of recent years had already struck him very hard ; times were bad for him and were to grow steadily worse. No greater mistake can be made than to assume that Cromwell belonged at this, or indeed at any, time to the landowning plutocracy. Such families as the Wentworths, Holleses, Hampdens and Russells counted their revenues in thousands, and although the elder branch of the Cromwell family was for a time at least wealthy enough to rank with them, Oliver did not of necessity belong to the same social and political group as his wealthy uncle. He was never one of those professional hangers-on, in whom this period abounded, who were to be found perpetually hovering in the corridors of Woburn or Wilton on the watch for places and favours. He chose to live at Huntingdon on his own resources, in complete independence and almost complete obscurity.

Meanwhile, as his income dwindled his family

grew. Fourteen months after his marriage his
eldest son Robert was born, followed by Oliver
in 1623, Bridget in 1624, Richard in 1626, Henry
in 1628, Elizabeth in 1629. Before the birth of
this sixth child, his prospects had been still more
overcast by the collapse of his uncle's fortune and
the sale of Hinchinbrook. The influence of his
family in the county was at an ebb, and it was on
his merits alone that he was returned to Parliament in 1628 as the representative of the borough
of Huntingdon.

In the troubled weeks during which this Parliament brought in and passed the *Petition of Right*
he played very little part. Only in the second
session, on February 11th, 1629, when the discussion turned on the recent innovations intro-
duced by the High Church Bishops whom the
King favoured, he rose to speak. All he could
add to the debate was an anecdote illustrating the
way in which his own old schoolmaster, Doctor
Beard, had been reprimanded for opposing the
" flat popery " of the innovators. Seventeenth-
century Parliaments were well used to anecdote
as a form of argument and Cromwell's delivery
seems to have had a rough impressiveness,
although his matter was lamentably dull, for at
least three of those present made a note of what
he said.

The debates on religion were barren. When the
Speaker, obedient to the King's will, attempted
to prevent further discussion a group of young
members, chief of them Denzil Holles, pounced
upon him and forcibly held him to his chair while
the House passed resolutions against Episcopacy.
This rude action brought King Charles' patience to
an end. He dissolved Parliament by proclamation
and determined henceforward to rule without it.

Cromwell's hand had not been with Denzil Holles, even if his heart had, which was as well for his family, since Holles and his confederates went to prison, pending the King's pleasure. For the next quiet years Cromwell's path and Holles' lay far apart : they were to cross again, to run for a while parallel, and at last widely to diverge.

The eleven years of the King's benevolent, aspiring and insolvent despotism, absurdly miscalled the " Tyranny," were spent by Cromwell in the pursuance of his private affairs, punctuated by incursions into local politics. In 1630 the burgesses of Huntingdon petitioned for a new charter, by which the administration was to be confined to twelve aldermen and a recorder, chosen to hold office for life, with a mayor chosen annually from among the aldermen. Cromwell was one of the substantial citizens of the town who agreed to this arrangement and was appointed a Justice of the Peace under it. He was one of the first to break the peace. Deciding on more careful consideration that the constitution was unjust, he criticised the Mayor so frankly that he was sent for to explain his conduct before the Privy Council. In the light of later events, the incident is interesting, for it reveals in full operation three of Cromwell's most essential characteristics – his tendency to act on impulse, his violent temper and his preference for an attack on an individual rather than on an idea.

His next activity, which followed close upon the other, was to intervene on behalf of his old schoolmaster, Doctor Beard, who was now advancing in years and anxious to appoint a successor to his place in Huntingdon. His request was not favoured by the High Anglican clergy about the King, but with the support of the local gentry,

among whom Cromwell was prominent, the old
man gained his point and died shortly after in the
happy knowledge that the people of Huntingdon
were not to be deprived of a teacher of sound
doctrine.

Cromwell in the meantime had left the town,
for in May, 1631, he gave up the unequal struggle
to live on the profits of wheat, and sold his land
for the modest sum of £1,800. To this period
belongs the story of his intended emigration to
America ; like the tales of his wild youth, it is
indifferently substantiated, yet it may have some
basis in fact. All the same, in spite of the apparent
triumph of the King's episcopalian views and of
Doctor Laud's " flat popery," Cromwell managed
in the end to square his conscience with the idea
of remaining in his native land. It was not to
New England, but merely to some grazing land
at St. Ives that he at length removed.

With this removal his fortunes reached their
lowest ebb. He now no longer owned his land,
but rented a farm, a distinction which in the
seventeenth century, with its rigid social conventions, meant much. His fall in society and his
stay at St. Ives were alike short. In 1636 his
maternal uncle, Sir Thomas Steward, made him
his heir, and soon after he moved to Ely, to take
possession at last of a considerable estate and a
comfortable income. Very wealthy he was not,
but after the struggles of the last years his position
was at last secure.

With a family which now consisted of his wife
and mother, four sons and two daughters, he
began his life again as a citizen of the cathedral
city in the fens. Possibly his wife's health had
suffered under the strain of so much house-keeping
and child-bearing. A son born in 1632 had died

within a few days, and not until the family had moved to Ely were the two youngest children born, the " little wenches " of whom their father was so often to think during his weary campaigns. In February, 1637, Elizabeth Cromwell gave birth to Mary, in December, 1638, to Frances. This was her ninth and last child : she was forty years old.

Cromwell's residence at Ely witnessed his third incursion into public affairs during the King's personal rule. The occasion was the enclosing and draining of the fen country, undertaken by the Earl of Bedford and a group of " gentlemen adventurers." While nobody denied that the drainage scheme would profit the district, Bedford and his partners, not only disregarded the popular privileges of fishing and fowling in the fens, but even infringed the property rights of smallholders. The part which Cromwell played in this complicated business has been the subject of much controversy, but there seems no doubt that he did defend the peasant and the smallholder against the engrossing capitalist. Later his enemies spitefully nicknamed him " King of the Fens," and the title had some justification in the popularity which he enjoyed locally.

Meanwhile at Ely he was a member of what was known as the Parson's Charity for giving relief to the sick and poor. These are straws of knowledge, indeed, yet not without significance in building up a picture of an honest and independent gentleman farmer, who showed his faith in the practical work of helping the afflicted and championing the poor. That his behaviour was often muddled and ill-considered is clear from the incident of the Huntingdon Charter. He had not yet learnt the ruthless controversial tactics which were later to stand him in good stead.

He had now reached the age of almost forty without distinguishing himself in any way. By the standards of his time, he was already well advanced in middle age. His sons, who were being educated at Felsted School, near his wife's home in Essex, were fast growing up. The eldest, Robert, was already sixteen when he succumbed to one of those mysterious and rapid fevers which decimated seventeenth-century households.

Although, long after, Cromwell was to speak of the shattering grief which this loss had been to him, he was sustained in the hour of trial by a firm faith in Providence. About a year before, in October, 1638, he had written to a friend praising the great mercies of God with a newly uplifted heart : " He giveth springs in a dry barren wilderness where no water is. I live, you know where – in Meshec, which they say signifies *Prolonging* ; in Kedar, which signifies *Blackness* ; yet the Lord forsaketh me not. . . . Praise him for me ; pray for me, that he who hath begun a good work would perfect it in the day of Christ."

What torments of doubt had preceded the revelation of which Cromwell spoke in this letter must remain for ever uncertain. There is evidence that during the years at Huntingdon he had been subject to fits of melancholy. Like many Puritans, he had allowed the idea of that harsh God, in whose shadow he had grown up, to prey upon his mind.

Not merely the Presbyterian group, to which Cromwell never belonged, but all English Puritan doctrine was tinged with Calvinism. The basic tenet of this faith is the belief in predestination : a man's soul is saved neither by faith nor by works, but by grace alone. Many were the Calvinists and Presbyterians, many were the more independent yet Calvinistic thinkers – of whom Cromwell was one – whose waking hours were tortured by the doubt of their own salvation. It was therefore no simple discovery of the essential goodness of God, no revelation of Christ's message, which pierced the darkness in Cromwell's soul. Rather it was the profound conviction that he was saved ; as he himself put it, that his soul was " with the congregation of the Firstborn."

It cannot be too strongly emphasised that to the great majority of Cromwell's Protestant contemporaries, in England and abroad, such a conviction was neither odd nor self-righteous. Indeed, all men of the Calvinist, Presbyterian, Baptist and generally " Puritan " sects devoutly prayed for such a conviction as this, both for themselves and their friends. Still less was there anything unusual in the belief which henceforward governed Cromwell's actions – that he was directly guided by the Divine Will. He did not, of course, regard himself as the infallible interpreter of God's wishes, but he tested his actions no longer by the criticism of other men, but by their own effectiveness. If he did God's will, he must succeed : failure meant that the divine contact had somewhere broken down – that there had been sin. This it was which gave him his buoyant confidence when things went well, and submerged him in such black despair in times of difficulty.

The processes of the human brain are never simple, and those of so active and introspective a mind as Cromwell's, saturated with Biblical knowledge, were exceptionally complicated. Yet the character of Cromwell was cast in great and simple lines, and in his character the root of all his actions is to be found, whatever tangled crop of reasoning he himself might throw up to obscure it.

By the time he was forty his character was formed beyond alteration. Such as he was in 1639, before he entered the open field of history ; such he was nineteen years later when, as Lord Protector of Great Britain and Ireland, he died. The essential features were all present in the farmer of Ely – the impulsive love of justice, the honest over-confidence in his own opinions, the rough and moody temper, the generous heart and that impregnable faith in the God within his breast which nothing now could shake.

CHAPTER II

HAD there been no Civil War in England, Cromwell would have passed the last twenty years of his
life as he had done the first forty, in reputable
obscurity. Sincerity and a blunt utterance might
have secured him a minor influence in Parliament
as the years went on, while his conscientious
attendance to his duties enhanced his local reputation. But he had neither the ambition nor the
clear-sightedness to become a political leader in
an undisturbed time. In argument he thought
slowly and moved clumsily, wielding theories
with the awkwardness of unfamiliarity. Crisis
alone, and crisis of a peculiar kind, was to reveal
the unexpected talent which forged him his way
to fame. His genius as a soldier, by the ines-
capable sequence of events, made him in time the
greatest power in England. But in 1639, if Cromwell knew one end of a musket from the other, it
was probably as much as could be said for his
acquaintance with military theory. Nor in 1639
did it seem probable that he would ever need to
know more.

What caused the apparently smooth surface of
England to split into those ugly fissures through
which the flames crept up to devour the land?

Three problems, so far unsolved by King and Parliament, were to cause the war. The first was administrative, the second economic, the third religious. The first was the problem of administration : what services was the State to give its subjects, how were they to be organised and who was to pay for them ? The second was the problem of financial control : could actual wealth be divided indefinitely from political power ? The third was the problem of religion : was the land to be united in a single Church, and in *what* Church ?

The third and last problem seemed to the men of the seventeenth century far more significant than either of the others. It was the open and stated problem. The other two were but implied in word or action, and left for the research of after generations to lay bare. And indeed, the revelation of these underlying problems, when it came, so intoxicated certain writers that for a time the whole idea of the *Puritan* revolution was consigned to the scrap-heap as an exploded theory, and religion was scoffed at as a blind used simply to cover an economic movement. Yet there is no reason to think the worse of our forbears because their actions, like our own, sprang from highly complex causes. Self-interest is the normal spring of human endeavour, and if it is sometimes the worse it is also sometimes the better for not recognising itself. To the great majority of the Puritan gentry who made the Civil War, our modern interpretation of their motives would be incomprehensible.

England in 1639 was ruled by a King with a lofty conception of his duty towards his people, who knew himself to be divinely appointed as the protector of their souls and bodies. Of the two he regarded their souls as by far the more important, an opinion fully endorsed by many of his subjects. Charles wished to save the poor from exploitation, to succour those in want, to reward the deserving, to maintain order and security throughout his lands. To achieve these ends, he had to rely on an administrative system based on the individual and unco-ordinated efforts of innumerable local officials – sheriffs, justices of the peace, vicars, masters of hospitals and almshouses, churchwardens, constables and beadles. The entire centralising organisation at his disposal consisted of two Secretaries of State and the Clerks of the Privy Seal and Signet. The Secretaries of State managed between them, indifferently, foreign and military affairs as well as English. The Clerks of the Privy Seal and Signet lived on nominal salaries, swollen by innumerable perquisites and petty exactions to a size sufficient to support them, with their wives and children. They were adept at extracting fees, and indeed thought of very little else. In these circumstances it is hardly remarkable that the central administration kept up only an intermittent and wholly inadequate communication with the local officials on whose goodwill the execution of the King's ordinances ultimately depended.

Working with such instruments, it was astonishing that King Charles achieved anything at all. In fact, he started a very creditable postal service, pulled the Navy into shape, and even managed to get the neglected Poor Law functioning better than it had ever done before – better, but not well.

Had Charles attacked the problem at the roots and set about a constructive scheme for co-ordinating local government and tightening the central control, it is possible that he might have made more of his long opportunity as an absolute ruler. But it is more possible, in fact probable, that he would only have plunged the country into civil war several years earlier than he did. The local gentry, in whose hands administration virtually lay, resented the least attempt to tamper with their authority, and indignantly called it an assault on private liberty and constitutional freedom. They may have been selfish, but they were not wrong in this. They had no guarantee that the central power would use its authority well, and when it did, it was an individual instance which did not invalidate their theory. In any case, Charles' tinkering with the problem was not successful enough to justify itself; he evoked resentment with one section of society without evoking any parallel popularity with another.

Closely linked to this administrative problem was the financial question. A central administration demanded far greater resources than any which Charles could command. The fact that the landowners who controlled local government also controlled the economic wealth of the country, still largely agricultural, was a trump card in their hands. The King, who could raise money continuously and effectively only by vote in Parliament, was bound hand and foot to the whims of the gentry who composed it. By the second quarter of the seventeenth century they were fully conscious of this fact.

Should the King attempt to govern without Parliament, his government would be insolvent, therefore inefficient, and therefore, in course of time, unpopular. In the last resort he must come back to the Commons for money. The supreme power, in theory in the hands of the King, was in fact theirs. Very soon the true state of the case would have to be recognised.

Hence, then, the suspicion and anxiety among the landed class when Charles, using every kind of financial subterfuge and questionable expedient, managed to prolong his independent rule from three, to five, to seven, to ten and at last to eleven years without calling a Parliament. It was beginning to look as though he would be able to continue thus indefinitely. And what then would become of the landed gentry and the power which they had learnt to use and to enjoy?

In the light of modern knowledge it would be absurd to deny that this growing terror among the landed gentry was the natural outcome of a selfish desire for power. It is equally absurd on that account to refuse both dignity and sincerity to their motives, and to deny that they sought power with a genuine intention of using it for their country's good. John Hampden, when he refused to pay Ship Money, defended the interests of his class with a total disregard for the equity and necessity of that un-Parliamentary tax. But the principle for which he stood, rightly understood, was a valuable one. Liberty of the subject, at any given period, inevitably means liberty of a particular class. But a principle is not necessarily vitiated because its practical bearing is limited. Even to-day it is an open question whether the liberty of a section of the community is in fact more or less liable to abuse than the impartial subjection of the whole.

Knit closely with these two problems of finance and administration was the religious question. Charles, like all rulers of his time, believed himself responsible for the welfare of his people's souls. The care of a soul, unlike that of a body, costs

relatively little. Moreover, the King had in this
sphere a centralised and highly efficient organisation ready to his hand – the Anglican Church.
Here, then, he was able to do efficiently what he
could not do in any other field. He was able to
probe into the very recesses of his kingdom, to
order, regulate and interfere, and to bring all
under a benign but rigid control. Here he came
up against two different but equally violent groups
of opponents : first, there were those who believed, like him, that the saving of souls was a
matter for the universal and dominant control of a
single organisation, but did not agree with the
tenets of the Anglican Church ; secondly, there
were those who vehemently asserted the right of
the individual to chose for himself. The first
group were the Presbyterians, the second the
sectaries, later to be broadly grouped as Independents. Both were classed together in the
popular speech of the time as Puritans.

This religious resentment, vocal in all sections
of the community and strong in the landed
gentry, submerged the other main problems and
swept them up together into one gigantic and
irresistible explosion against the Crown.

Rebellion came first in Scotland. Charles sent
for his ablest Minister, Strafford, to rescue him
from his troubles. Too late he made a bid for
popularity by calling the Parliament of April,
1640. But no feeling against the Scots could be
evoked among the Commons and after three
weeks Charles dissolved the assembly. He had
gained nothing save a knowledge of his peril.

Cromwell, who represented the borough of
Cambridge in this brief gathering, must by this
time have been watching the progress of events
with anxious interest. His education and his

conversion made him one of those to whom liberty
of conscience was essential. The Scottish revolt
was breathing life into the latent opposition of
England ; the future of religious freedom depended on the stand now being made across the
border, and the success of that stand depended,
in part at least, on the support of England.

About midsummer, 1640, the Scots invaded
England. Strafford had counted on the invasion to
provoke a reaction in the King's favour, but he miscalculated. Charles' subjects would not help him.
The Army was mutinous, the country sullen, and
the gentry refused to subscribe to the nation's
defence. By August the King was forced to make
a truce. The collapse of his policy drove him once
again to call a Parliament and by the beginning
of November, 1640, Cromwell, again returned for
Cambridge, was at Westminster.

The May Parliament had shown the more
vigorous members of the House of Commons that
the way lay open to them. The King had failed
to organise a party for himself. Decisive and
immediate attack would overthrow his Ministers
and put the control of future policy in the hands
of the Commons. John Pym, the ablest and
boldest of the Puritan group, speaking to some of
his supporters at the opening of the new assembly,
declared that " they must now be of another
temper than they were the last Parliament." To
this ardent Puritan group, led by Pym, Cromwell
belonged.

The House of Commons, as we have seen, was
dominated by the landed gentry. London and
some of the ports were represented by merchants
and there was a growing group of lawyers, but it
would be a mistake to suppose that these two
sections differed in interests and outlook from the

Cc

landed class. Almost all of them, whatever their profession, had a connection with the land. Merchants had bought country estates, just as landowners had frequently invested in trade. Many of the lawyers had a stake in the land in the shape of some small property, and almost all the rest were the younger sons or near relations of landowners influential in the districts which they represented in Parliament. Over and above all, connecting and soldering together the whole of this ruling class, were the indissoluble bonds of seventeenth-century marriage ties.

The landed gentry of England included families of such wealth as the Wentworths, the Russells, the Hampdens ; but the majority of those who were to be most active in Parliament were neither the scions of these great houses nor their hangers-on, but the rank and file of small independent men – men like John Pym and Oliver Cromwell.

Cromwell was in fact a typical member of the Parliamentary class. He was a small landowner, married to a merchant's daughter, whose family had in turn invested in land. The marriages of his own and previous generations of Cromwells gave him no less than eighteen kinsmen in the House of Commons in 1640. Of these the most important were John Hampden, the hero of the Ship Money case, and Oliver St. John, both ardent supporters of Pym.

Yet to Cromwell, as to many of his colleagues, the religious question was of far greater importance than any theory of constitutional reform. The attack on Charles' policy and Ministers, the repeated and triumphant assertion of Parliament's financial control and the assault on the judicial and executive powers of the Crown were but preliminaries to the reform of religion. The grea

issues of political toleration and freedom of sp
were incidentals in a campaign which was
secure liberty for tender consciences.

Cromwell, a comparatively silent member of
earlier Parliaments, was active from the beginning
of this new gathering. On November 9th, two
days after the King opened Parliament, Philip
Warwick, strolling into the House in all the consciousness of elegance, directed a maliciously dis-
approving eye towards the large red-faced man
who was speaking. He noticed that the gentleman's linen was indifferently clean and that his
suit had been made by a country tailor. Nor did
he like the contents of his oration. Cromwell was
speaking in favour of John Lilburne, whom the
King's Court of Star Chamber had whipped and
imprisoned for distributing John Prynne's libellous
pamphlet in the streets. We do not know why
Lilburne had turned to Cromwell to bring his case
before the Commons. Yet it is strange that thus
at the very outset of his career Cromwell came
into contact with this man : this was not the last
time that he was to be concerned with the doings
of the noisy and fearless democrat.

Henceforward Cromwell's activities increased.
Although he played no part in the impeachment
of Strafford, the most important immediate con-
cern of the Commons, he was on several Committees, and on December 31st moved the second
reading of William Strode's Bill for annual Parliaments. Six weeks later he had a sharp passage
with the Royalist Sir John Strangways, in which
he openly attacked the established Church. Resentment of government interference in matters
of conscience was already the fundamental basis
of his political thought, and in April, 1641, he
once again bore witness to his views by demanding

the exclusion of the Bishops from the House of Lords.

By the end of the summer of 1641 the Commons, under Pym's acute management, had undermined the royal power. They had broken the King's direct judicial power, assured their control of the revenue and deprived him of the right to dissolve the present assembly or to govern without Parliamentary consent. Nothing was left to the King save the control of the Army. Pym, early exponent of the approved technique of revolution, now stretched out his hand for this last and deadliest weapon. In August, 1641, a Committee of Defence was appointed by the Commons in order to consider who should control the trained bands, the ordnance and the strong places of the kingdom.

Revolt in Ireland and a bloody attack on the English settlers in Ulster came to increase the tension between the King and the opposition. The Commons doubted not merely Charles' competence to quell the rising, but his honesty. Their suspicions were further aroused by his inept attempt to sow dissension between his English and Scottish opponents. When the Commons met again after the recess, on October 20th, 1641, they proceeded to draw up that well-known manifesto against the royal government called the *Grand Remonstrance*.

The general dislike of Strafford, whose arrogant capability had made him few friends, and the sincere belief that long intermission of Parliaments was a threat to the constitution, had given Pym a working majority in the Commons for the opening months of his campaign. With Strafford dead and Laud in prison, many of Pym's original supporters grew indifferent or even hostile. This was particularly true of Anglican constitutionalists like Edward Hyde, apostles of appeasement like Falkland or wealthy moderates like George Digby, who saw nothing to be gained by a general upheaval. Had there been an organiser of genius in this group, who could have stolen the leadership of the Commons from Pym, the history of England would have been different. But the active minority who still upheld Pym were better united in their Puritan fanaticism than the moderates in their tepid desire for settlement, and this minority comprised the greater number of the striking personalities of the House – popular Hampden, impassioned Strode, fiery Holles.

That Pym's supporters comprised the wealthiest section of Parliament is a fallacy. The allegiance of the Russells and Herberts was at this time still doubtful. The Sackvilles and the fabulously wealthy Comptons were Royalist; so were the Cravens, descendants, like the Comptons, of a Lord Mayor of London. Those who have much to lose are not commonly found among the advocates of extreme policies, and Pym was nothing if not an extremist. His policy aimed, if not at war, then at a breach with the King and a shattering defeat of royal pretensions by a well-defined constitutional settlement. The risk of civil war on such an issue was immense. Pym did not hesitate to take it.

The debates on the *Grand Remonstrance* served to show which of the Commons were ready to follow Pym to the logical end of his endeavours. It was carried after vehement argument by a majority of eleven. Pym's position was still tenable, but it was no longer secure. Day by day that fluctuating fringe of waverers which had given him the casting eleven votes might melt away. Determined to force the issue quickly, he encouraged his supporters to yet more open attacks on the King. Before the year was out Sir Arthur Haselrig brought in a Bill for taking the command of the militia and trained bands out of Charles' hands. Rumours that the Queen was to be impeached penetrated to Whitehall.

On January 4th Charles realised that only a show of successful force could now save him. He set out from Whitehall with a troop of horse to arrest the five most obstreperous members of the Commons – John Pym, John Hampden, Arthur Haselrig, Denzil Holles and William Strode. Forewarned, they escaped by the river and Charles, marching in too late, cut a poor figure. Nothing is more laughable than a *coup d'état* which fails.

From that moment peaceful settlement was impossible. Unable to defend their cause in debate at Westminster, Charles' leaderless supporters, both in Lords and Commons, abandoned London and followed the King himself to the north. All the spring and summer of 1642 the opposing parties gathered strength, King and Parliament sending out rival commissions for recruiting soldiers, and each attempting to secure the ports and fortresses of the land. Towards the end of April Charles tried to enter Hull ; the governor closed the gates in the name of Parliament. War had begun.

CHAPTER III

THE MILITARY PROBLEM : 1642–1644

Cromwell's activities in Cambridge – Battle of Edgehill –
military theory and practice of the time – Cromwell's
theories – Eastern Association – Battle of Winceby – Cromwell's religious policy at Ely – death of Cromwell's son –
Parliament allies itself with the Scots.

DURING these last critical weeks Cromwell had
been active. On January 14th, 1642, he had
proposed the appointment of a Committee to put
the kingdom in a posture of defence. A little later
he offered out of his own comparatively small
resources, £600 for the reduction of the Irish
rebels and £500 for the defence of Parliamentary
rule in England. The summer found him in his
own county busy organising its defences. He
seized the magazine at Cambridge and prevented
the despatch of the college plate to the King. In
the late summer he received his captain's commission from Parliament, while his eldest surviving
son, Oliver, now nineteen years old, took up arms
as a cornet.

In July Parliament had appointed the Earl of
Essex commander of its army. A soldier, with
some reputation acquired in the Low Countries,
Essex had been prominent among the opposition
to Charles in the House of Lords. He did not
doubt that the King could be brought to abandon
an unpopular policy by a display of force, but he
was no republican, and of overthrowing monarchy, or even this particular King, he had no
idea.

At this time Cromwell also believed in the

authority of King in Parliament, with the
emphasis on the latter. But his politics played a
secondary part. He saw chiefly that the King
must be made to allow freedom of conscience to
his subjects; all other concessions forced from
him were but subsidiary to this. As for the way
to this ultimate goal, Cromwell saw it step by step
as he followed it. His was not the temperament
to worry overmuch about the day after to-morrow.
From first to last he solved his difficulties as they
arose, and singly. The first problem now was
the successful waging of a war.

England was fairly evenly divided between the
two parties. Parliament had the advantage of
possessing the capital and held the greater part of
the eastern and south-eastern counties, while the
King was strongest in the midlands and the west.
On August 22nd Charles unfurled his standard at
Nottingham. By mid-October the Royalists were
advancing across the midlands, intending by way
of Oxford, now in the hands of a small Parliamentary force, to strike the London road.

In Warwickshire Essex, with the main body of
the Parliamentary army, attempted to cut them
off, and in a strong position on the Edgehills over-
looking the village of Kineton the King gave
battle. The engagement, bloody and indecisive,
resulted, thanks to the vigour of his young cavalry
leader, Prince Rupert, in a strategic gain for
Charles. He took Oxford, pushed on and might
have entered London had he not been checked at
Turnham Green. Baffled, the Royalist forces fell
back to the university city, which now became the
King's headquarters.

Cromwell had been present at the latter part of
the Battle of Edgehill, although he had not taken
part in the deadliest of the fighting. He had used

his brain as well as his sword, noticing how Rupert's charge went through the unstable ranks of the opposing cavalry, and seeking to find the reason and the remedy. Going straight to the root of the matter, he spoke his mind to John Hampden. " Your troops," he said, " are most of them old decayed serving-men and tapsters and such kind of fellows : and . . . their troops are gentlemen's sons, younger sons and persons of quality . . . you must get men of a spirit that is likely to go on as far as gentlemen will go : or else you will be beaten still." John Hampden's agreement to this statement, even according to Cromwell's account of the interview, was of that perfunctory kind which is commonly given to persons who state obvious but irremediable truths.

Cromwell was not the man to abandon the idea merely because its realisation seemed impossible. He set himself, if not absolutely to remedy the type of recruit, at least to evolve some method by which the material ready to hand could be made serviceable.

The significance of the theories which he now evolved becomes greater when they are considered in the light of contemporary military practice. The only experienced soldiers in England had been trained in Germany and the Low Countries. Of the Royalists, Wilmot and Goring had served under the Prince of Orange, the nominal commander-in-chief, Lord Forth, under the King of Sweden. Of the Parliamentary commanders, Essex had seen some, although very little, service in the Low Countries ; the elder and the younger Fairfax rather more. But the pressure of continuous war on Europe had modified out of recognition the theories of discipline and organisation laid down by such masters of military theory as Maurice of Orange and Gustavus of Sweden. Armies were composed of mercenaries without convictions. Prisoners of war habitually took up arms for their captors, and when pay failed plunder automatically took its place. Towards the end of the Thirty Years' War, now in its last decade, a reputable Swedish commander did not even contract to pay the new recruits : they were expected to make their own living by licensed robbery.

Trained soldiers who took service in England soon discovered that conditions were different. In the first place, prisoners had to be provided for, since in a war fought largely out of conviction the troops did not, in the early years at least, change sides with the automatic ease common abroad. The extreme inadequacy of the arrangements made for prisoners is in itself eloquent of the inexperience of even veteran commanders in dealing with such a problem. Besides, in England the civilian, for whose alleged rights the war was being fought, was far more important than in any European country. The people had to be conciliated, not quelled, and Prince Rupert, who began by demanding blood-money from the town of Leicester in the fashion universally approved and practised by every commander in the German wars, was firmly ordered by his uncle to give it back. The management of the troops on both sides was marked by phenomenal consideration for the feelings of the civilians; the discipline of Prince Rupert's cavalry for instance, in spite of the charges brought against it, compares favourably with that of any of the commanders in the German war, the King of Sweden not excepted.

It was Cromwell's great virtue that he added to

an exceptional gift for organisation a complete ignorance of the demoralising foreign influences to which the professional officers automatically subscribed. To read the letters of Cromwell after those of a Torstensson is to step into a world where the values have altered.

In the winter of 1642–3 the Eastern Association, or league of counties, was formed, which under the command of Cromwell and the Earl of Manchester soon proved an effective weapon against Royalist disaffection. The counties of Hertford and Huntingdon were brought under control and the headquarters of the Parliamentary troops fixed for the time being at Cambridge. Meanwhile by active recruiting Cromwell converted his original troop of horse into a regiment.

In the first flush of enthusiasm, the Commons offered to provide not only pay but equipment for the recruited men, an arrangement which doubtless much assisted Cromwell in his early struggles. But very soon money gave out. By April, 1643, he was already lamenting that he had exhausted his private means, was in sore need of pay for his men and could get nothing from London. But, unlike the professional commanders, he was far from accepting the position as inevitable or indeed reasonable. He had raised his troops on a system of his own and was determined that they should be honourably treated. " If you choose honest godly men to be captains," he wrote, " honest men will follow them." This was a singularly unorthodox method of recruiting, but Cromwell stood to it. His intention was to have men individually and corporately conscious of the cause for which they fought, so that their dogged resolution would match the fire of their opponents. By asking and expecting the impossible, he almost got it.

Noticeably there were few foreign-trained officers
among his own troops. His captains, like himself
were amateurs, learning by immediate experience
– and that, in a country as unused to war and in
circumstances as unorthodox as the English
conflict, was, if anything, an advantage.

Cromwell's letters are more full of the honesty
and godliness of his troops than of their military
skill, but he had not neglected this side of their
training. His careful drilling and instruction
bore early fruit. At the end of April, after
disarming the Huntingdonshire Royalists, he
re-took Crowland ; on May 13th he defeated a
superior number of Royalist cavalry near Grantham and before the end of the month had pushed
forward into Nottinghamshire. He was now
ready to join forces with the two Fairfaxes in the
divided county of Yorkshire, where they were
struggling to establish the ascendancy of
Parliament.

Treachery brought the plan to nothing. The
Governor of Hull, that same Sir John Hotham
whose defiance of the King had initiated the war,
was now in correspondence with the Royalists.
The vigilant Cromwell discovered his plotting
and helped in the denunciation and arrest which
brought Hotham and his eldest son to their death
on Tower Hill. But for the time being the
northern advance had to be abandoned.

In the late summer and early autumn the troops
of the Eastern Association renewed the campaign.
Cromwell with Manchester and Lord Willoughby
reconquered Lincolnshire, advancing from the
south, while the younger Fairfax and some of his
troops joined them from the north. On July
28th, 1643, Cromwell took Gainsborough, and
on October 13th seriously defeated the cavalry of

the Lincolnshire Royalists at Winceby. At this engagement, during which his horse was killed under him, Cromwell first decisively proved the new spirit of his men. Their fame began to spread rapidly in the enemy ranks.

In the meantime Manchester had been named commander-in-chief for the Eastern Counties, with Cromwell as one of his four assistant colonels. He was in fact, if not in name, the second-in-command and in October he was given the responsible post of the governorship of the Isle of Ely. Cromwell was too able a subordinate to be easy to work with, and his disapproval of the lazy and self-seeking Willoughby culminated in a complaint to the House of Commons which led to Willoughby's resignation. Up to this time he appears to have agreed fairly well with Manchester : several months were to pass before he was to try the same methods with more far-reaching effect on his chief commander.

Cromwell did not forget his ideals in the business of fighting for them. He strenuously kept up the standard of godliness among his troops and used his first important appointment to further the cause of the Puritans. As Governor of the Isle of Ely, he not only gave free licence to new sects, but within a short while suppressed the Anglican service in the Cathedral. Marching into the lofty building one January day in 1644, he summoned the officiating clergyman to quit the building. The priest, bold in his own way and not to be put out of countenance by one of his own parishioners, continued to intone. " Leave off your fooling and come down, sir," shouted Cromwell. And with that made an end of singing in Ely Cathedral for the next sixteen years.

It was shortly after this that young Oliver died

suddenly of a fever at Newport Pagnell, where he
was with the garrison. Cromwell's eldest child
was now the angular and austere Bridget, whose
soul storms found their way even into the pages
of her father's letters. The eldest surviving son
was the incorrigibly indolent and good-natured
Dick.

Political events usurped the time which might
have been spent in grieving. The winter of
1643-4 brought a change in Parliamentary policy
which was to be decisive. Pym had died at the
end of December, leaving as his legacy to the
Parliamentary cause a newly-signed treaty with
the Scots. Their alliance had been essential to
turn the fortunes of war. The arms and men
which they were in a position to give would
weight the scale in Parliament's favour, particularly in the divided north. Feeling immediate
help to be more important than ultimate concessions, Pym had bought Scottish friendship by
agreeing that the English Parliament should subscribe to the Solemn League and Covenant and
impose the Presbyterian religion on England
when the war was won.

Although he died before the final completion
of this obligation, Pym had rightly calculated the
feelings of his fellow Parliamentarians. Even
those who were not in sympathy with the rigid
organisation of the Presbyterian Church felt that
Scottish help could not be too dearly bought.
Only one member of the House of Commons, Sir
Ralph Verney, refused to take the Covenant.
Some others, it is true, postponed the act for as
long as possible, among them Cromwell. As a
true believer in liberty of conscience, he could
not whole-heartedly accept the teaching of
Calvin and Knox. But the time had not yet come

for argument : that could wait until the King was defeated.

Yet both in Parliament and army a fissure was already there, beneath the surface, ready to split the united front from end to end as soon as the pressure of war should be removed. On one side was the Presbyterian group, who genuinely wished the terms of the Scottish treaty to be put in force. Chief among them was Denzil Holles. On the other side were those who, like Cromwell, had been ready to bargain for Scottish help, but were not ready to pay the full price for it after it was won. From the signing of the Scottish treaty the party later to be so widely and fearfully known as the " Independents " had come into being, and Pym, bequeathing a strong coalition for war to the Parliamentary cause, bequeathed also the schism which was to make the war of no avail.

CHAPTER IV

THE MILITARY PROBLEM SOLVED : 1644–1646

Siege of York – mission of Sir Harry Vane – Battle of Marston Moor – Cromwell attacks Crawford – second Battle of Newbury – Cromwell attacks Manchester – *Self-Denying Ordinance* – Cromwell General of the Horse in the New Model Army – Battle of Naseby – collapse of the Royalists – fall of Oxford.

In February, 1644, immediately after the signing of the Scottish treaty, a Committee of Defence for Both Kingdoms was set up, to membership of which Cromwell was appointed. His activity in the field continued, nevertheless, to be of more value than his advice on committees. Early in January the Scottish army under Lord Leven, a veteran of the German wars, crossed the Cheviots, deep in snow, making towards York. Cromwell, who had passed the earlier part of the year stamping out abortive Royalist movements in Buckinghamshire, joined Fairfax in May at the siege of Lincoln and proceeded thence across the Yorkshire border to join with the Scots in the siege of York.

The Royalists defended the city with great valour, knowing that a strong relieving force under Prince Rupert was on its way from the south. During the intermission of warfare the Parliamentary generals meanwhile received Sir Harry Vane, a leading member of the republican group in the Commons. He had come to lay before them a scheme for the deposition of the King. It was rejected outright by the three chief commanders, Sir Thomas Fairfax, Lord Manchester and Lord Leven.

Cromwell's opinion of it is unknown, but a coolness with Manchester seems to have started at about this time. Nevertheless, tension with Manchester cannot be taken as definite proof that Cromwell had differed from his superiors in this matter of Vane's plan. He was always suspicious of Parliament's noble and wealthy supporters. His own officers were often artisans and small tradespeople, and he had hounded Lord Willoughby mercilessly out of his command because he did not think that he was in full sympathy with the ideals of the party. But if Cromwell was not at this time, nor for some time to come, a republican, yet he regarded Charles' deposition as a solution not to be left wholly out of account.

For the time being, military events forced political disputes into the background. Prince Rupert, a strategist of acknowledged distinction, who had meanwhile organised the King's cavalry into a flexible and deadly weapon, skilfully outmanœuvred the besiegers and raised the siege of York. Fearing that their retreat would be altogether cut off, the besieging army fell back to Tadcaster. Rupert, harassed by news of the King's difficulties in the south, decided to pursue them on the chance of putting their army completely out of action before returning to the rescue of the King at Oxford. About seven miles to the south-west of York, on Marston Moor, the two armies faced each other, Prince Rupert taking up his ground with his cavalry about nine in the morning on July 3rd, and the infantry under Newcastle joining the main body of the army all too slowly during the course of the day. The Parliamentary army were less ready for the ordeal, and

Dc

Fairfax, sending desperately for the return of the
Scots, who had drawn off northwards, was
rejoined by Leven only when the day was half-
spent.

Newcastle's sloth prevented the Prince from
making a surprise attack on the retreating army,
and the two forces were now bound to the more
perilous alternative of a pitched battle, Rupert's
18,000 men being heavily outnumbered by the
27,000 of the Parliament and the Scots. In the
circumstances, the Prince drew up the first line
of his cavalry in a remarkable position, fronting
the muddy lane which straggled across the moor
between the two armies and having in front of
them a deep ditch. It was clear from this arrangement that the Prince did not intend to initiate the
conflict. Should the opposing forces attack – he
knew that he had Cromwell to face and was on
his mettle – he meant to act on the defensive, with
the help of the ditch which should break the force
of the enemy's charge. Far out on the right flank
he had placed a reserve of cavalry which was to
close in on Cromwell when his troops were fully
engaged in front.

On both sides there was some argument as to
the order of the day, Rupert asserting his authority
over a recalcitrant Newcastle not without difficulty, while on the Parliamentary side the two
wings of horse and the foot in the centre tended
to operate as detached units. Cromwell was on
the Parliamentary left, with his own Eastern
Association cavalry and a considerable reinforcement of Scots. The effective command on that
side was his, although Leslie was technically the
senior officer.

The day was damp and heavy, and towards six
in the evening although the sun was not to set

for three hours yet, the darkness of a rising thunderstorm made the light so uncertain that all the King's commanders agreed that the likelihood of any action that day could be disregarded. The Royalist lines broke up for supper. At that moment Cromwell charged.

Even then the recovery of the opposing forces was quick and the Prince might have made good his defensive tactics had not his reserve on the flank, instead of waiting until Cromwell was fully engaged, intervened before the two forces had closed and fatally hampered their own side. It was the only time in the war that Cromwell and Rupert, each in his own way an outstanding cavalry general, met each other face to face. And in spite of the initial advantage Cromwell's victory was very dearly bought. Rupert rallied his men, brought in his second line with shattering effect and for about half an hour it seemed uncertain which way the conflict would go. But then, wave upon wave, came Leslie's Scots breaking against Rupert's now undefended flank. Outnumbered, without a reserve on which to fall back, the Royalist cavalry began to give and then, with the spreading sense of hopelessness, to scatter. By seven o'clock they had been driven off the field.

Victorious on his own side of the field, Cromwell now turned to see how the fight went elsewhere. On the far side Fairfax had been driven off the field by Goring, but Goring's cavalry, thinking all was well with their friends, were pursuing the defeated troops and showed no sign of coming back before night-fall. In the centre the Royalist infantry held the opposing forces in check, locked in a struggle of which the issue was still uncertain. All therefore depended on the use made of his victory by Cromwell, Leslie and the cavalry on the Parliamentary left. It was then that Cromwell executed that brilliant and dangerous move which won the battle for Parliament. Turning his troops and re-forming them in the now failing light, he swept across the middle of the field between the Royalist infantry and the reserve and took up his stand on the farther side of the field in the position held by Goring at the beginning of the struggle. The King's infantry, thus surrounded on all sides, died fighting. They had no alternative. Some of Goring's cavalry, returning too late to relieve their comrades, fell themselves into the hands of the victors, among them Sir Charles Lucas, Newcastle's cavalry general. Of the King's men, 4,000 had been killed, 1,500 taken.

" God made them as stubble to our swords," Cromwell wrote afterwards. And Rupert was the last to underestimate his victor ; it was he who in the hour of defeat gave him the name which was to remain with his men, " old Ironside." Marston Moor was a turning point in the war : it lost the north for the King and it established the reputation of Cromwell's cavalry.

During the first charge Cromwell had been grazed by a bullet on the neck, which seems momentarily to have stunned him. But, contrary to the vicious scandal broadcast by his jealous colleague, Crawford, and published by Denzil Holles, he recovered himself in time to play the leading part in the rest of the engagement which is commonly and rightly ascribed to him.

He had suffered a personal loss in the battle, and two days later from the camp before York he was writing to his sister's husband, Valentine Walton : " Sir, God hath taken away your eldest son by a cannon-shot. It brake his leg. We were necessitated to have it cut off, whereof he died. Sir, you know my trials this way. . . ." It is the only reference in all his letters to the death of young Oliver.

Meanwhile in the south and west matters went less well with the Parliamentary forces. Waller complained bitterly of the badness of the troops in Hertford and Essex, and in Cornwall the Parliamentary infantry was cut off and forced to surrender at Lostwithiel.

If the news from the south was bad, Cromwell was not satisfied with affairs in the north. Manchester failed to take advantage of Marston Moor, and Rupert immediately showed that he was not to be quelled in a single fight. Other commanders, Newcastle and Lord Eythin, might fly the country, giving up all for lost. The Prince collected his scattered forces and recruited new troops in his retreat across Lancashire into Wales, issuing out again to join the King with troops less demoralised than avid to retrieve their laurels.

Moreover, the religious cleavage in the Parliamentary party was growing serious. Cromwell's reputation as an Independent and the " darling of the sectaries " made him enemies among the Scots and Presbyterians, both in the army and at Westminster. He for his part was growing suspicious of Manchester's intentions. The Earl made it obvious, by his bewildered and dilatory conduct after Marston Moor, that he was embarrassed at the prospect of utterly defeating the King. He knew that Charles would still be King, whoever won the war, and was anxious for a settlement before matters had gone to extremes. Otherwise, so thought Manchester and his kind, republicans like Vane and fanatics like Cromwell

would be destroying the traditional privileges of
the nobility.

Cromwell opened his campaign against Manchester by a personal attack on Crawford, the
Scottish professional whose lack of personal conviction was a perpetual stumbling-block.   The
dislodging of Crawford proved harder than he
had anticipated, and finding it difficult to sub-
stantiate his objections to him, Cromwell altered
his tactics and placed before the House of Commons the more general complaint that the war
was being mismanaged.   Manchester, momentarily forced into a corner by these insinuations,
was compelled to agree to prosecute the war to a
final conclusion against the King.   Having won
his point, Cromwell reverted to the religious
question and persuaded Parliament to set up a
Committee to enquire into and settle the differences between Presbyterians and Independents.
If the differences could not be settled, means were
to be found to tolerate the Independents.

Cromwell's actions were reasonable enough. It
was natural to want to know the intentions of a
commander as important as Manchester. It was
reasonable to seek a settlement of the religious
questions which threatened the stability of the
Parliamentary cause. But the Presbyterian party,
and more especially the Scottish divines in session
at Westminster, were incensed at this interference.
Knowing the resolute determination of General
Cromwell, they were not unjustified in feeling a
certain apprehension.   Meanwhile in the Lords
feeling ran very high against him. He had undermined Willoughby and was undermining Manchester.   The position of a House of Lords, in
revolt against the King, equivocal in itself, needed
careful guarding.

Manchester, gathering his spirits, countered Cromwell's attack by accusing him and " his juncto " of spreading unrest in the army by indiscreet and impulsive words.

Events in the field hastened the outbreak of a second storm at Westminster. At Newbury, on October 27th, 1644, Cromwell was once again in action under Manchester's command. He was probably by this time in a mood to disapprove of anything which Manchester did. But in fact the engagement was shamefully mismanaged on the Parliamentary side, and Cromwell was justified in ascribing his failure to dislodge Prince Maurice from Speen Heath to Manchester's inefficient co-operation.

On November 25th, Cromwell opened his final attack by accusing Manchester to the House of Commons of shameful and persistent negligence. Incensed past enduring, the House of Lords retaliated by setting up a Committee to enquire into the conduct of General Cromwell. This was a signal for a fight between the two Houses on the question of privilege, each accusing the other of infringing its rights. Under cover of this minor conflict, Cromwell, whose political tactics seem to have acquired something of the skill of his military manœuvres, beat a strategic retreat, in order to bring up his batteries against a weaker place. On December 9th he announced that it would be more profitable to discuss remedies for the army's inefficiency than its causes. He was willing, he stated, to believe that the Earl of Manchester had been guilty of nothing worse than accidental oversights. The debate, for which his speech set the tone, closed with a vote that henceforward no member of either House should be eligible for a military command.

This was the beginning of the so-called *Self-Denying Ordinance*, which, by ridding the army of irksome political divisions, was to end the war.

After seeing the Ordinance through its initial stages, Cromwell once more left the verbal battle-ground of Westminster for the field. The early spring of 1645 found him in the west under Waller's command – and behaving with exemplary subordination.

Meanwhile at Oxford Rupert, too late given the chief command over all the King's armies, was with ill-supplied and dwindling forces preparing an offensive for the coming summer. In April Cromwell was sent to prevent his leaving Oxford, but Rupert eluded his watch and broke through to Leicester. The town fell almost at once and the Prince pushed on across the midlands in a desperate attempt to reach the Associated Counties and break up the solid front of the Parliamentary defensive.

By the *Self-Denying Ordinance*, Cromwell's commission expired on May 13th, unless he should be re-elected. Three days before it expired the House of Commons extended it for six weeks. It was hardly a moment at which they could afford to lose one of their best officers. Early in June the Londoners petitioned the House of Lords to send Cromwell to the defence of the Associated Counties. This demand was followed almost immediately by an appeal from Fairfax, now commander-in-chief of the so-called New Model Army, that Cromwell might continue as General of the Horse. On June 10th Parliament agreed that Cromwell could remain in the army for as long as the House of Commons could dispense with his services.

His position thus sanctioned, Cromwell joined

Fairfax on July 13th, 1645, in Northamptonshire, a few miles from Market Harborough. The Royalist Council of War, overruling Prince Rupert, had decided to manœuvre for a battle. Even before Cromwell joined the army, Fairfax had the greater numbers. With Cromwell's troops added, the King's army was outnumbered by two to one. By then it was too late to withdraw. The battle which took place on June 14th near the village of Naseby is a landmark in the constitutional history of England, but from the military point of view it was uninteresting. It did not need Cromwell's genius to win a battle at those odds, and even the complete collapse of the Parliamentary left wing, commanded by Ireton, under the impact of Rupert's first charge, did no more than sway the issue for a few moments. Cromwell, who had only the insufficient and half-mutinous forces of Sir Marmaduke Langdale to deal with on his side of the battle, must inevitably have driven him off the field, even if the Royalist infantry in the centre, confused by a mistaken order, had not thrown the whole of the King's army into disorder. The rout was complete, the slaughter horrible and the barbarities committed by some of Cromwell's men on the women of the vanquished, even though he was not himself responsible, are a stain on his memory and a blot on the otherwise glorious name of the *Ironsides*.

Naseby settled the outcome of the war, although with dogged obstinacy the Royalists fought on. Cromwell and Fairfax overran the west. Goring was driven out of Langport on July 10th ; Bridgwater, Sherborne, Bristol, Winchester, Basing House and Longford fell before the winter came. In the early spring of 1646 what was left of the King's western army capitulated at Truro. Cut off on every side, Oxford held out until the following midsummer, almost a year to the day after the catastrophe of Naseby. The King fled northwards and gave himself up to the Scots. Rupert, after negotiating the surrender of the city, sailed for the Netherlands. The first Civil War was over. If Cromwell had not himself won it, it could not have been won without him.

CHAPTER V

ARMY, KING AND PARLIAMENT : 1646–1649

Cromwell's point of view – tension between Parliament and Army
– dominance of the Independents in the Army – unsuccessful
attempts at mediation – the Army seizes the King – and
marches on London – Cromwell's negotiations with the
King – and with the Army officers – flight of the King –
Cromwell's opinion hardens against Charles – Second Civil
War – siege of Pembroke – Battle of Preston – Pride's Purge
– trial and execution of the King – Cromwell's motives and
justification.

THE twenty-two months which divided the surrender of Oxford from the outbreak of the second
Civil War were a crucial period in Cromwell's
career. On the interpretation of his actions at
this time depends the interpretation of his whole
character.

There is room for legitimate doubt of Cromwell's genius. His military triumphs were too
much the result of special circumstances to place
him among the great soldiers of the world,
although his influence with his men, his tenacity
and his imaginative handling both of tactical
and psychological problems would have distinguished him anywhere. His subsequent
achievements as a statesman will always be the
subject of controversy. But of his profound sincerity there can be no serious question. His
letters and his career, approached with a reason-
ably open mind and a sympathetic knowledge of
seventeenth-century thought and diction, put it
beyond doubt.

Oxford fell eight years after Cromwell's conversion ; he had guided his conduct through the

wars always by that conviction of God's will working within him, which he then acquired. His men went into battle singing religious songs, and each soldier carried with him a little pocket edition of the Psalms, done into English verse, which Pym's half-brother had compiled and which is used to this day in Scotland. It had served Cromwell's turn to imbue his troops with this practical religious feeling, to choose godly captains and impress upon his men that they were indeed fighting the battles of the Lord. But it served his turn so well only because he himself believed in what he preached. Louder and more confident grew Cromwell's trumpet-call of faith, resounding through his letters. "With this handful it pleased God to cast the scale," he had written after the fight at Grantham in 1643. At Marston Moor came the triumphant "God made them as stubble to our swords." At Naseby a wondering, almost awe-stricken joy in his victory : "This is none other but the hand of God."

By the end of the war Cromwell's religious confidence had swollen to gigantic proportions. "I advised you formerly to bear with men of different minds from yourself," he had written once angrily to Crawford – advice which he frequently gave to others, but rarely followed himself. He was patient only with opinions which could be reconciled with his own, and he met direct opposition by instantly and sincerely invoking the Almighty. Cromwell's understanding was good and he had not the bitter fanaticism of many of his party. But his sympathies, broad-based as they were, were incapable of intellectual enlargement and points of view which had been beyond his compass in 1638 were beyond his compass to the end of his life. He grew in practical experience, in knowledge of men and in self-confidence ; but he had come into the open field too late to change the habits of half a lifetime. When he laid down his burden at fifty-nine, he was a sadder, a wearier, a more experienced man than when he took it up at forty-one : but he was not more understanding.

The end of the war left a political situation of baffling complexity. The people in general wanted peace, and had never wanted anything else. But Parliament controlled the settlement of terms and at Westminster the intransigent Presbyterian group was in command of the situation. Under their direction the Prayer Book was superseded, and above 2,000 Anglican clergy deprived of their livings. Among the neutral gentry and peasantry – the great majority by this time – there was an immediate and indignant reaction in favour of King and Church.

While Parliament pursued this unwise policy, ill-feeling began to spread in the Army. The *Self-Denying Ordinance* had had time to take full effect in the year which followed Naseby. The type of officer and soldier favoured by Cromwell was now in the ascendant. The severance of Parliamentary and military positions had increased the Independent element in the Army at the expense of the Presbyterian and the indifferent. In the infantry, raised still by casual recruiting, by pressing and even by desertions from the other side, strong feeling was on the whole confined to the officers. In the cavalry it was prevalent in all ranks. The Army had become a nursery for extreme political and religious views, sown in time of war, and springing into multitudinous growth in the idleness of peace. The Army which had won the war for Parliament now threatened Parliament itself.

Thomas Fairfax was still commander-in-chief, a
post which he retained until the summer of 1650.
A distinguished professional soldier, he had
neither the political skill nor the religious
fanaticism to control the Army in time of peace.
Cromwell, several years older than he, was the
dominating force. At his side another figure was
emerging, the harsh Ireton, who had married
Bridget Cromwell, many years his junior, in the
camp during the siege of Oxford – a romantic
setting for this unromantic pair. As the situation
developed it became apparent that the Independents in the Army were further subdivided into
two main groups ; there were the purely religious
Independents, like Cromwell and Ireton, who were
uninterested in the political application of their
moral theories, and there were those who carried
their beliefs into other spheres and demanded the
radical re-organisation of society. This group,
later to be known as the Levellers, derived their
chief inspiration from John Lilburne, the prolific
journalist, whose cause Cromwell had pleaded six
years earlier before Parliament. It is superfluous
to labour the point that the first group comprised,
on the whole, men of substance, while the second
was recruited chiefly from the ranks and from
men of the people. The Cromwell-Ireton group,
fundamentally conservative, believed in monarchy.
The Levellers did not. This antagonism, too, was
to play its part.

In spite of Cromwell's difficult views, the Commons had speedily rewarded him for his services.
When offering terms of peace to the King before
Oxford fell, they had asked for an estate for him to
the annual value of £2,500 and a barony. In
February, 1646, they settled such an estate on him
themselves, out of the lands of the Marquis of

Worcester. Yet the ill-feeling against Cromwell in the Presbyterian group grew stronger. The Scots even hinted that he had given Oxford unduly lenient terms because he wanted to reach a private understanding with the King.

The German wars, now smouldering to an end, could offer several examples of popular generals who had dictated their own terms to the civil authority. Mutinous armies had forced their will on protesting diplomatists and baffled rulers, regardless of the state in whose pay they fought. The situation in England, with a large unpaid army, hostile to Parliament, was ugly in itself, and looked uglier in the light of contemporary events abroad.

Meanwhile the Commons were weakened by internal division. The *Self-Denying Ordinance* forbade any member of the House to hold a commission except in special circumstances, but it had not prevented the reverse process of an Army officer obtaining a seat in the Commons. The local elections held in 1645 and 1646 to replace excluded Royalists had brought in many Army officers – Hutchinson, Harrison, Ireton, Ludlow, Fleetwood, to name only a few of the most eminent. They were a sensible reinforcement to the ranks of Parliamentary Independency. It is apparent from the policy of the Commons, during the year which followed the surrender of Oxford, that the Presbyterian party, while still numerically stronger than the Independents, had to be sure of a good attendance before it could force its measures through. There were waverers and the ascendancy varied from day to day.

The relations of Army and Parliament centred on two problems. In the first place, would the Commons be able to raise the money necessary to

l an army long unpaid? In the second
vould they carry out the promises made in
ber, 1644, when toleration had been
guaranteed to sectaries outside the Presbyterian
Church? On the night after Naseby Cromwell
had written to Speaker Lenthall of this promise.
"He that ventures his life for the liberty of his
country," he wrote, "I wish he trust God for the
liberty of his conscience, and you for the liberty he
fights for." It was a little muddled in expression,
perhaps, like so much that Cromwell wrote in
heat and haste, but the meaning was clear.

Now that the fighting was over, Cromwell
sought only two things – the liberty of conscience
for which the war had been fought and decent
treatment for the soldiers who had fought it.
Four years of experience with harassed Commons
and callous professionals had not made him go
back on the words he had written in 1643 : "I
have a lovely company . . . they expect to be used
as men." So far he was staunch in his loyalty to
Parliament. "I can speak this for my soldiers,"
he had written early in 1645, "that they look not
upon me but upon you : and for you they will
fight, and live and die in your cause." He
believed this to be true when he wrote it and for
long after. Only by degrees did he become convinced of what Parliament already suspected –
that the troops did not trust in the Commons and
were not loyal.

Parliament, lacking both the money to disband
the troops and the desire to countenance every
outrageous sect which had grown up in the ranks,
handled the situation disingenuously and badly.
At the New Year of 1647 the Scots handed over
the King to their keeping. With this royal
prisoner, with the legislative and the executive still

in their hands, they had almost all the cards, but they had no skilled leader. Holles, whose stinging eloquence was effective in opposition, had neither true state-craft nor a good sense of the situation.

The Presbyterian element in the Army had dwindled, but not disappeared. By emphasising their religious views in dealing with the soldiers, Parliament might have managed to split the ranks against themselves. But instead they advertised their inability to pay, and threatened to disband the Army save for a small minority which was to go to Ireland. They also unwisely encouraged civilians, the Londoners in particular, to complain of the troops.

" God," wrote Cromwell, " is in Heaven and He doth what pleaseth Him : His and only His counsel shall stand, whatever the designs of men and the fury of the people be." He had need to appeal to Heaven for the situation was fast passing out of his control. Over-confident of his own powers, he had thought during the spring of 1647 to use his personal influence to secure an accommodation between Army and Parliament. He genuinely feared the consequences of rebellion on the part of the Army against the highest constitutional authority in the land – the two Houses at Westminster. But he was human, and he may as genuinely have seen the way to acquiring extraordinary powers and prestige by constituting himself the architect of the new peace. Ambition, however little he himself recognised it, can hardly have been absent from his plan, although it was certainly not the dominating consideration. His whole political outlook prompted him in the direction of a settlement between Parliament and the troops.

Cromwell's   military   judgment   was   not

E<small>c</small>

paralleled by a keen sense of a political situation, nor, it would seem, by any very profound knowledge of men. From the early days at Huntingdon he had had a habit of hurling himself into a conflict without envisaging the probable reactions of his opponents. So it was in the spring of 1647. He miscalculated both Parliament and the Army. Both sides immediately suspected his good faith. Lilburne, in a pamphlet called *Jonah's Cry*, openly accused him of betraying the Army's cause and the people's liberty by his mild attitude in Parliament. The Commons, on the other hand, were determined to be rid of him as a dangerous sectary, and brought in a measure to prevent any but Presbyterians from holding commissions.

Suspected by both sides and seeing no way out, Cromwell for a brief moment contemplated taking service abroad. Events bore him onwards before he could escape. The spokesmen of eight regiments – " adjutators " as they were called until popular speech slurred it into " agitators " – appealed to Fairfax and Cromwell to lay their cause before Parliament. Growing frightened, the Commons empowered the generals to discuss the Army's grievances with the troops. The concession came too late, for the hopes of the extremists rose as Parliament showed signs of weakening. On May 20th, 1647, Cromwell reported to the House that he thought the troops would disband, but it was useless to think of sending them to Ireland. The Commons thanked him for his services in the usual polite formula. But they were not feeling polite. By this time they were frightened, and as frightened of Cromwell as of anyone else. They fancied that he knew a great deal more about the unrest in the Army than he admitted.

His actions during the next fortnight bore out
their worst suspicions, for it was at this time that
he made the first of his rapid changes of policy.
He recognised the impossibility of a settlement,
and, throwing his previous hopes and theories
overboard, now sided emphatically with the
Army. Sincere the change undoubtedly was;
he knew – none better – what Parliament owed to
the troops which it was prepared to treat so badly.
Moreover he had given his first mistaken policy
some months of trial – enough to prove its worth-
lessness. But if Cromwell can be defended from
the charge of hypocrisy on this score, he cannot be
acquitted of political instability. All that can be
said is that in politics as in arms he was an
individualist, a law to himself.

On May 31st Parliament ordered the troops to
disband and told Fairfax to hand over the
artillery. Fairfax refused and sent for Cromwell.
Meanwhile in London Cromwell had consulted
with other Army officers in his house in Drury
Lane, and from thence had given orders to Cornet
Joyce to go to Holmby House, where the King
now was, and prevent Parliament from moving
him to London. His flair for immediate necessities
made it clear to him that in the open struggle now
beginning between Army and Parliament the
personal control of the King might well be the
trump card. Immediately after, on June 3rd, he
left London. Not a minute too soon. Parliament
was already planning to lay hold of him as a
traitor.

The tables were turned on Parliament. The
King, without whom neither party contemplated
a settlement, was the Army's prisoner. Cromwell,
once again certain of his immediate plan, exploited
his dominating personality to restore order among

the troops. The agitators were relegated to the background and a Council of War, on which he was himself the dominating member, took charge.

His policy during the next months was directed at securing the agreement of the King to a settlement pleasing both to the Army and the Independent elements in the Commons. Having abandoned his original idea of an accommodation between Presbyterians and Independents, he was now prepared to sacrifice the Presbyterians altogether to the Independents and the Army, provided he could get the King to accede to their interests. Here again, as events were to prove, he miscalculated his men. The Leveller element in the Army refused to trust the King and very soon again refused to trust Cromwell. He and Ireton found their dealings with the King interpreted in a singularly unpleasing, if not an absolutely false, manner. Far worse than this, Cromwell failed entirely to understand Charles. He did not realise that the King had been waiting for the split in the ranks of his enemies which was now so hopefully apparent, and would play off one group against the other to the best of his ability; not forgetting, either, to continue clandestine negotiations with the Scots. Charles is hardly to be blamed for his disingenuous policy during the summer and autumn of 1647. Each group was trying to outwit the other and Cromwell was no more honest than anyone else. The subterfuges in which he indulged to secure the support of the united Army on the one hand, and of Charles on the other, have only this to be said for them, that he believed them to be divinely inspired. Later on he was to recognise that something very strange had gone wrong with his divine inspiration during that summer and autumn of 1647.

On June 10th, meanwhile, he informed Parliament that the Army sought nothing but justice, and would not meddle with the constitution. Five days later the Army belied his asseveration by issuing a *Declaration* asserting its own sovereignty as the true representative of the people, and demanding the expulsion of Denzil Holles and ten others from the House of Commons. For the next weeks the Army officers continued their negotiations with the King, not unhopeful of a settlement. But the City of London, predominantly Presbyterian and suspicious of what was going on in the Army, precipitated a crisis. The apprentices rioted, broke into the House of Commons and silenced the Speaker, while Holles and his party passed resolutions against the Army. Immediately Cromwell marched on London.

He was met on the way by the Speakers of both Houses and many of the Independent Members, and on August 6th the Army marched through the city, to accompanying shouts of " Lords and Commons and a free Parliament ! "   It was a strange way to make Parliament free, by expelling Holles and his more active friends, and settling the Army within convenient threatening distance at Putney. Cromwell can hardly have deceived himself as to the probable outcome of all this. " What we gain in a free way," he was to say later, " is better than twice so much in a forced way." From now onwards the " forced way " alone was left.

By elevating the Army at the expense of the Commons, Cromwell precluded the possibility of a constitutional agreement and rendered void the political causes for which the war had been fought. He was to prove in his career the truth of that biblical dictum that those who take the

sword shall perish by the sword. He himself did
not perish, but those principles for which he had
fought were destroyed by the military force which
had been set up for their protection. By ethical
standards Cromwell was wrong in thus arrogating
to himself and the Army a supreme power to
which they had no claim. Judged on the narrower
standard of expediency, it is hard to see what else
he could have done, at that time and in those
circumstances, to avert national disaster.

The problem was however far from solved, and
as Cromwell pushed on in his effort to win the
King for a settlement in the Independent interest,
his position became more and more untenable.
Charles played for time, negotiating with the
Scots, and Cromwell, urging him to accept the
proposals laid before him by the Army in preference to those suggested by Parliament, did not
realise that the King's apparent compliance was
a subterfuge.

Meanwhile, his own and Ireton's intentions
were suspect in the Army. His son-in-law, an
immensely eloquent, compelling, narrow-minded
man, who stood on his own dignity as an officer
and a gentleman, was not popular. It was clear
that whatever constitutional settlement he and
Cromwell wanted, it would take little note of the
aspirations of the now growing party of the
Levellers. Lilburne continued to pour out his
vituperative, democratic pamphlets. The soldiers
gathered together in groups talking religion and
the equality of men. Cromwell and Ireton, whose
continual doings with the King were more and
more unpleasing to the republicans, would not be
able to control the Army much longer unless a
definite decision were reached.

In October, 1647, the extremists confronted

Cromwell and Ireton with the first *Agreement of the People*, a document demanding radical franchise reform, biennial Parliaments and the dissolution of the present assembly. On October 28th a general council was held at Putney with the intention of making some reconciliation between the point of view of the Levellers and of Cromwell and Ireton. It was at this meeting that Ireton, who was certainly the mouthpiece and some thought the inspiration of Cromwell's policy, came out with a rigid defence of property rights and of the sanctity of contracts. As against this, Colonel Thomas Rainborough stood out for constitutional reform and manhood suffrage. Neither Rainborough nor Ireton was easy to handle, but Cromwell, who in a dispute of this kind showed at his best, managed to prevent the debate from becoming too acrimonious and a temporary reconciliation was effected.

For his own part Cromwell was wholly out of sympathy with Rainborough's views. His religious convictions had never been of that adventurous kind which overthrow all the conventions of society. His preoccupation with the individual soul never led him to the obvious belief in the absolute equality of men. The prejudices of the middle-class landowner were too deeply imbedded in his nature to be eradicated by argument. Souls might be equal before God, but incomes and responsibilities were not. He was as genuinely hostile to the economic and political equality advocated by Levellers and Fifth Monarchy Men as he was to the spiritual tyranny of the Anglicans.

The limitations of Cromwell's political thought thus prevented the inception of an advanced constitutional experiment. Now, as later, he was

re concerned to re-establish a firm basis for
vilian life than to test extravagant theories. He
had fought for liberty of conscience, and in so far
as politics had entered into his calculations at all,
he had thought more of curbing what he considered to be an unorthodox increase in the royal
power, than of initiating radical change. In the
stress of war he had considered the idea of remov-
ing the King, should all else fail ; but even here
political necessity, not republican theory,
prompted his belief. As things now stood, on
the other hand, political necessity seemed to
indicate the re-establishment of the King under
specific control.

This conservative position of Cromwell's, midway between the King and the Army, had grown
untenable, when Charles himself put an end to the
deadlock by his attempted escape in November,
1647.

The King's flight, while it relieved Cromwell of
the impossible burden of further negotiations,
placed him in an invidious position. Whatever
settlement had been arranged, Cromwell, as its
architect, could not have failed to gain some
personal advantage. The idea had certainly not
been repugnant to him, and to Cromwell's ingenuous pleasure at the thought of increased
power, must be added Ireton's frank ambition.
Rumour said that Cromwell had been bribed with
an offer of the Earldom of Essex, and a pamphlet
of that autumn declared that " these promising patriots were but sweet-mouthed courtiers."
Very shortly after, when matters turned out
differently, another group of Cromwell's enemies
started the theory that the negotiations had been
nothing but a blind to trap Charles, by alternate
hope and fear, into making the desperate and

unsuccessful attempt at escape which put an end to the discussions and virtually signed the royal death-warrant.

That Charles' flight helped Cromwell out of an impossible situation there is no doubt : but he could hardly have planned the whole elaborate network of plot and counter-plot in which the King is alleged to have been caught, he could hardly have arranged chances and time sequences so aptly unless he had been even more closely in the confidence of Heaven than he himself believed.

The first to reap advantage from Charles' flight were the Scots. Cheated by the English Army and Parliament of their just rewards for winning the war, the Scots had reopened negotiations with the King. His flight left him with no other friends to whom to turn. In December, 1647, he signed the *Engagement*, by which he called in the Presbyterian Scots to restore him to the English throne.

Meanwhile indignation in the Army was directed alike at Charles and Cromwell. Only by undertaking to redress all grievances and thoroughly to reform the Parliamentary system did Cromwell manage to bring the troops to order again. A mutiny at Ware in Robert Lilburne's regiment – he was " noisy John's " brother – was instantly quelled by Cromwell in person. Before the end of November an uneasy calm had been restored in the Army.

By that time Cromwell's own views had undergone their second and last radical change. He threw overboard his policy of negotiating with Charles as ruthlessly as he had previously thrown over his policy of conciliating Parliament. In the immediate outstanding problem, the problem of the disposal of the King, he found himself at last in agreement with the republicans. The change was not so quickly effected as the change of the early summer had been, for here it was not merely a policy but a whole principle which was at stake. A conservative, Cromwell always in his heart clung to monarchy, not as a sacred institution, but as a reasonable form of government. His anger was directed against a man and not a theory. In this he differed radically from the republicans ; the difference, important later, was trivial in the winter of 1647.

Different theories have been put forward to explain this change of front. The King's flight, shocking as it was to Cromwell's susceptibilities, was not in itself final. Intercepted letters revealing the extent of Charles' commitments to the Scots and his evident intention of re-establishing himself even at the cost of a second war, seem to have turned the scale at last against him in Cromwell's baffled mind. At a council of officers on November 11th, when Harrison asked that the King be proceeded against to the last extremity as a " man of blood " who had deliberately deceived the peace-makers, Cromwell hesitantly conceded that " if it be an absolute and indisputable necessity for us to do it," then it must be done. From that time onwards his conviction of the necessity of destroying the King seems to have grown.

In December the Army Council met at Windsor to compose all dissensions. True to their beliefs, the officers held a great fast day on December 23rd, Cromwell and Ireton praying devoutly with the rest. To a mind adjusted to prayer, like Cromwell's, the processes of thought are eased by such solemn appeals to God. Not long after the fast day a new note of certainty rings out again in his words and letters. In the Commons he spoke of the King as " an obstinate man whose heart

God had hardened." He told the House that the Army would stand by them only for so long as they carried out their duties to the country : should the Commons fail in this, then the Army would fend for itself.

As the outcome of this speech the vote of *No Addresses* was passed, by which negotiations with the King were broken off. He was now close prisoner, with no other hope in the world save in the Scots army and the projected rising of the English Royalists. Thus, two months after Charles' flight, Cromwell had forced the final breach with the King. If it had been his intention to make such a breach from the first, it was a remarkably slow consummation for so elaborate a plan.

At the same time Cromwell refused to enter into any definite engagement as to his future actions, in spite of pressure from the republicans within Parliament and without. Lilburne, active and indignant as ever, burst out with an accusation of treason against him. These civilian denunciations, while they provided a background of worry, did not affect the Army, which grew in unity as the danger of a second war and a Scots invasion became imminent. Cromwell, who had been seriously ill and absent from public business in the early spring, was back at his post in April, 1648, when a new fast and prayer meeting was called at Windsor, lasting this time for three days. The officers were now all at one in condemning those " carnal conferences " with the King, held in the previous autumn.

In May the storm broke, with risings in Wales, the Home Counties and the north, followed by a Scots invasion. Hastening first to Wales, Cromwell reduced Pembroke Castle after a siege of six weeks. Hence he marched to join Lambert in

Lancashire just in time to check the Scots' advance. Internal trouble in Scotland robbed the invading army under Hamilton of support from that country. In a three days' fight from August 17th to 19th, 1648, in the neighbourhood of Preston, Cromwell shattered the invaders. Hamilton was taken.

Fairfax in the meantime had trapped and starved out the southern Royalists at Colchester.

But the absence of the soldiers in the defence of the kingdom had given the Commons one last chance of asserting themselves. They reopened negotiations with the King, and the victorious Army found that the terms of a new pact, the so-called Treaty of Newport, had been arranged without consulting its needs or wishes. Cromwell joined in the general indignation of the troops. He had pledged his word that no peace should be signed without consulting the interests of the Army, and when his troops petitioned Parliament against the projected treaty, he forwarded their petition to Fairfax, asking him to give it his support. This done, he set out for London.

While he was still on his way, the southern army, no less indignant than the northern, took the law into its own hands. Colonel Pride stationed himself outside the House of Commons and refused admittance to all members notoriously out of sympathy with the soldiers. After the Purge of those two days, December 6th and 7th, 1648, a bare seventy members were left in the Commons.

On December 7th Cromwell arrived in London. He had taken no part in purging the House of Commons, but he accepted the accomplished fact.

Cromwell's behaviour in the ensuing weeks has been much obscured by slander, so that it is difficult to trace his actions. While his sympathies were wholly with the Army, yet he does not seem to have played so prominent a part as might have been expected. He was present at the Council of Officers on December 15th which decided that Charles must be brought to justice. His name appears, along with many others, on all the Committees of the House of Commons connected with the King's trial ; but the Journals of the Commons give no evidence of any particular or exceptional activity on his part. Sir Thomas Wroth was the member who moved that the King be impeached, and the High Court of Justice which was to try him was established formally by Act of Parliament on January 6th.

No less than eighty-eight persons of those nominated to try the King made their appearance at one or more sessions of this Court. Sixty-nine of these were members of the House of Commons and thirty-one officers in the Army, sixteen being both officers and members. The result of the trial, if trial it can be called, was a foregone conclusion. Only one man could have saved the King. Had Fairfax at this eleventh hour stood out for his own moderate and monarchist views, he might have had the power and popularity necessary to rescue Charles. He hesitated – and rightly – before plunging the country into yet a third civil war. Remaining himself outside London, he left his outspoken wife to hurl defiance at the King's judges.

Cromwell's actions were enigmatical. Up to the last moment he seemed half inclined to consider projects for sparing the King's life. Yet, in spite of this, during those last anxious ten days of January, 1649, while Charles was sentenced and the death-warrant signed, he used all his influence to rally the nervous and the waverers. Of the fifty-nine signatures which were at length obtained to justify the King's death, his own name stood third.

On January 30th, 1649, Charles died, with that royal calm and Christian resignation which cast a radiance over his life and sanctified his cause in a million hearts.

The Court of Justice and its actions did not in any sense represent the people's will. Suspicious, conservative and politically uninstructed, the people believed in monarchy and were shocked at the King's death ; but with the great majority, then as now, the next meal was of greater import-ance than the most stirring events of the political world. They had soon forgotten all about it.

Cromwell was acting in the best interests of the people in so far as he realised that only through Charles' destruction could peace come to England. No compromise was possible and while Charles lived no settlement would hold. By all the canons of right and wrong as he understood them, Charles who had cheated his captors when they gave him terms, and provoked a second war, deserved death. It was plain justice, and in all his remaining life Cromwell never thought of it otherwise.

And, indeed, although judicial murder is a cold and horrible thing, it is hard to see why Charles' death should draw so much pity from posterity. For the radiant youth of Lord Bernard Stuart, trampled to death at Rowton Moor, for the democratic idealism of Thomas Rainborough, pistolled by his Royalist captors at Pomfret, for thousands dead on the battlefields, shot in reprisals, starved and plagued away in prisons, an impartial world might well have more regret than for the King. Stupid, aspiring, well-intentioned, stiffly convinced of the rectitude of a political theory which he would not, left to himself, have had the wit to invent, Charles cannot be defended. It was his misfortune, not his fault, that he lived to be a King : it was Cromwell's misfortune that he had to be rid of him.

Cromwell's conscience was never, so far as we know, to trouble him for Charles' blood. He had had no choice in the matter and as always he took the strong political compulsion for the voice of God. He, and many of those who stood by him in this bitter business, did indeed feel a conviction which posterity should respect, even if it cannot understand it. Eleven years later Thomas Harrison, speaking at his trial for high treason before the judges of the restored monarchy, his cause broken and his life in hazard, was to call again on that authority, higher than the King's, to which alone he owed obedience and under which he had acted. " I followed not my own judgment," he said, " I did what I did as out of conscience to the Lord." He spoke for Cromwell.

CHAPTER VI

ARMY AND PARLIAMENT : 1649–1654

House of Lords abolished – mutiny of the Levellers – the first
Irish campaign – the second Irish campaign – the first
Scottish campaign – Battle of Dunbar – the second Scottish
campaign – Battle of Worcester – the Dutch War – tension
between Army and Parliament again – political ideas of
Cromwell and Vane contrasted – Cromwell expels Parlia-
ment – the Little Parliament – resignation of the Little
Parliament.

ON January 4th the House of Commons had
voted " that the people are under God the original
of all just power." In this belief, sincerely held
if strangely expressed in his actions, Cromwell
had worked for the death of the King. He did
not attempt to reconcile it with the fact that the
House of Commons now consisted of a handful of
the Army's supporters, while he himself had no
intention whatever of enlarging the franchise.
Yet he did feel, when the crisis was past, that
something should be done to make the Commons
slightly more representative of the nation. He
accordingly secured an amendment in the declaration of loyalty that all members were now re-
quired to take, so that those who had had qualms
about the King's death could at least be re-
admitted to the deliberations of the House.

The tide had now set, not only against monarchy, but against ancient convention. On
February 6th the House of Lords was abolished ;
this was no very serious loss, for of the minute
handful of peers who remained the only two who
were still seriously concerned in contemporary

politics, Salisbury and Pembroke, immediately sought and obtained election to the Commons.

The King's death left the Army the source of all authority in England. But it was an unstable power, the outcome of events, not of a constructive plan, and therefore a prey to circumstances. The crisis of the second Civil War had brought the Army together again, but as soon as the King was dead the old difficulties re-emerged. Cromwell had killed the King, but he had not abandoned his traditional and conservative view of politics. All this latter part of his life he was to find himself torn between his own desire for a reasonable and even a conservative settlement and the revolutionary action forced on him by the times.

Now that the King was dead and Royalism temporarily broken, he wished to re-organise the country along the lines laid down by the revised *Agreement of the People* issued by the Army with his sanction on January 15th, 1649. This document, which provided for a limited franchise reform and the speedy dissolution of the sitting Parliament, was not to the mind of John Lilburne and the Levellers. No sooner was the King dead than Lilburne began his shouting once more and denounced the Council of State, now theoretically the chief authority in the country, as subservient and Cromwell as a hypocrite.

The King's execution had given new life to the extreme democratic elements in the country, and early in April a group of enthusiasts began to dig up St. George's Hill and plant rows of beans, thus giving practical proof of their theory that all the land in England belonged to the people. This demonstration, which met with more scorn than admiration, was comparatively unimportant. Far more serious was the unrest among the Levellers in the Army, now approaching dangerously near to mutiny. Cromwell did not underestimate the danger. " If you do not break them," he said, " they will break you."

In March, Lilburne, whose pamphlets were fanning the trouble in the ranks, was placed under arrest. But it was already too late. The discontent was too widespread, the democratic feeling too strong. In May mutiny broke out at Salisbury. The Levellers, nearly a thousand strong, marched across the Downs to Oxfordshire hoping to join with sympathisers in those parts. But they were disappointed, and when it came to a trial of arms, there was more talk than determination among them. Cromwell and Fairfax, pursuing their march and demoralising them with firm but generous appeals, soon brought over the greater number. Those that showed fight to the last were but a handful, soon destroyed. The highest officer among them, a captain, was cut down in a wood near Wellingborough making a last, desperate stand. Of the prisoners, a cornet and two corporals were shot, the two latter facing the firing party unrepentant, convinced that their cause was right – as indeed it was. In London John Lilburne was tried, and although the jury refused to find him guilty, the strength of the extremist party was for the time being broken.

The forces of tradition were too strong for Cromwell to have acted otherwise than he did. Already political circumstances had carried him into waters too deep to negotiate. Now, after the King's death, as nine years before, his first thought was still for religion. He, like many others, had attacked not the English constitution but the King's Church policy. The particular quality of

Charles' religious convictions had made it impossible to alter that policy without destroying him, and with him the constitution. Cromwell, therefore, who had no training in political theory, no taste for it, and no desire to experiment with it, was presented by circumstances over which he had no control with an opportunity for making gigantic constitutional changes. He neglected that opportunity because he had not asked for it, he did not want it and he did not know what to do with it.

All that he wanted in 1649, as in 1640, was security of government and liberty for tender consciences. For the revolutionary overturning of property rights, for the establishments of political equality between men, for the abolition of " the ranks and orders of men, whereby England has been known for hundreds of years " he had no desire. He saw in such ideas merely causes for the fresh disturbances which of all things he was most anxious to avoid. It is hardly fair to accuse Cromwell of insincerity because he so patently failed to carry the Civil War to a logical and revolutionary conclusion. Had he betrayed ideas which he had once held, the accusation against him would be serious : but he had never held any ideas which, to the modern mind, seem in the least politically advanced. The execution of Charles I, unlike that of Louis XVI, was to those that compassed it not a bloody demonstration of the people's rights, but an awkward political necessity. Cromwell killed Charles because he thought it was the only way to bring peace to England. He shot the Levellers for the same reason.

The next important problem to be solved by the English Government was the subjection of

Ireland. On March 15th, 1649, before the
outburst of the Levellers' mutiny, Cromwell had
been appointed to command the forces which
were to go there. On August 15th, 1649, he landed
in Dublin with 12,000 men. His coming was
followed by a drastic purge and re-organisation
of the Irish army ; plunder and blasphemy were
put down in an effort, not wholly unsuccessful,
to make the demoralised rabble in the service of
the Government something like the New Model
which Cromwell had done so much to create.

Two shattering campaigns in the late summer
and autumn of 1649 and the spring of 1650, saw
the collapse of Irish Royalism. The troops which
Ormond, commander-in-chief for King Charles II,
had at his command, were scattered and ill-
armed, and the defence was undermined by violent internal dissension. Cromwell and his
lieutenants swept all before them. Drogheda fell
on September 11th, Wexford on October 11th,
Ross on the 19th. Sickness forced Cromwell to
raise the siege of Waterford in December, but the
following spring he carried his arms inland from
the coast. In February he took Cashel and
Cahir, in March Kilkenny, in May Clonmel. The
remnants of the Royalist resistance scattered to the
four winds. By the early summer of 1650 the
quelling of Ireland could be safely left to his
lieutenants, of whom not the least was his son
Henry, at twenty-two one of the most promising
young officers in his army.

The first Irish campaign is a blot on Cromwell's
career which no specious justification can altogether efface. At the fall of Drogheda nearly
3,000 of the defenders had been killed ; at
Wexford hundreds of civilians had been put to
the sword. Cromwell defended himself against

accusations of barbarity by asserting with truth that he kept good order among his troops, allowed no plunder and was ready to redress any wrong done to those not actually in arms against him. The massacre at Drogheda was in accordance with that harsh rule of war – sometimes though not invariably enforced – by which a garrison which held out without reasonable hope of relief could claim no mercy. The massacre of the civilians at Wexford was partly accidental. Inexcusable in themselves, these barbarities seem worse from Cromwell's own ferocious glorying in them. " The Lord is pleased still to vouchsafe us his presence, and to prosper his work in our hands," he wrote, and spoke complacently of the " righteous judgment of God upon these barbarous wretches." Like most of his English contemporaries, he had believed and had remembered the atrocity stories circulated in England nine years before about the massacres of the settlers in Ulster. He saw himself now as the tool chosen by God to wreak vengeance on the perpetrators of " the most barbarous massacre that ever the sun beheld." It was a matter of indifference to him that the innocent must suffer with the guilty, and that the soldiers of Drogheda and the civilians of Wexford had not set foot in the scenes of the Irish massacres of 1641.

After the fall of Clonmel, Cromwell sailed for England, where Parliament was clamouring for his help. The Presbyterian party in Scotland, in one last effort to win back what they had lost through the triumph of Independency in England, had crowned the young Charles II king and were threatening to invade England. Parliament had wanted Fairfax to march against them, but he refused on the grounds that their army had not yet crossed the border. He would be willing, he said, to take command as soon as they invaded, but he would not seek them out in their own country.

Thus in June, 1650, Cromwell was made in name what he had long been in fact, commander-in-chief of the Army. " I have not sought these things," he declared ; " truly I have been called unto them by the Lord." He had in vain used all his influence to prevent Fairfax from resigning.

Cromwell crossed the Scots border at the head of about 16,000 men in June, 1650. The commander of the opposing army was that same Leslie at whose side he had fought at Marston, an experienced and cautious soldier. A month of manœuvres failed to draw the Scots into battle and at the end of August sickness in the ranks compelled Cromwell to withdraw to the plain of Dunbar, which he intended to use as a base for future operations. Leslie saw his opportunity and, by quickly outmanœuvring Cromwell, cut off the English between the hills and the sea. The Scots army numbered about 20,000, Cromwell's by this time not much more than half as many.

In this desperate position the God in whom he trusted once more stretched out his hand on Cromwell's behalf. Leslie, who seems to have thought that the English intended to embark on their provision ships and make the best of their way off, allowed himself to be persuaded to leave his strong position on the hills to attack Cromwell in the plain. Before the amazed eyes of the English army, the Scottish troops descended on to the flat ground. Cromwell was not likely to miss such an opportunity.

At dawn on the following day he initiated the conflict with a cavalry charge, the direction of which he left to John Lambert, while he himself conducted a movement designed to take Leslie on the flank when his front rank was already engaged. The Scots army, largely consisting of raw recruits, was no match for Cromwell's determined veterans. His cavalry proved, as always, irresistible. " The best of the enemy's horse being broken through and through in less than an hour's dispute, their whole army being put into confusion, it became a total rout : our men having the chase and execution of them near eight miles," he wrote that night to Speaker Lenthall. To his wife he wrote on the following day : " The Lord hath showed us an exceeding mercy ; – who can tell how great it is ! My weak faith hath been upheld."

Cromwell did not feel towards the Scots as he had done towards the Irish. " Since we came into Scotland," he wrote to Lenthall, " it hath been our desire and longing to have avoided blood in this business : by reason that God hath a people here fearing his name though deceived." After the Battle of Dunbar he was anxious to reach a compromise settlement, and his overtures met with a qualified success, for, although the King's supporters did not surrender, yet they were weakened by the desertion of many waverers, whose doubts of the wisdom of setting up Charles II were confirmed by the miracle at Dunbar.

Edinburgh surrendered on December 19th, 1650. But Cromwell postponed the spring campaign partly because he fell seriously ill and partly to allow time for further negotiations. Not until June, 1651, did he again take the field, and this time with the definite intention of ending the war before the autumn. The question of money was, as always, acute : Cromwell knew that another winter and spring of warfare would bankrupt the English Government. He therefore struck recklessly and successfully to force an immediate issue.

Pursuing Leslie northward to Perth, which surrendered on August 2nd, he left the road to England open to the King and the rest of his army. Having established garrisons to hold the country and left General Monck to pacify it, Cromwell turned to follow the King's inferior forces across England. He overtook them at Worcester and here, on September 3rd, the anniversary of the Battle of Dunbar, he destroyed what was left of the Royalist army. The young King and a few followers fled – after months of wandering to find refuge at last in Paris.

The last shot of the Civil Wars had been fired. Parliament voted an income of £4,000 a year to Cromwell, with Hampton Court for a country residence, and when he rode into London on his return from the campaign, accompanied by Speaker Lenthall, the streets were lined with cheering crowds. " The generalissimo," reported the Genoese agent to his Government, " will do what he pleases." The war was ended and the work of " settling and healing " could begin.

In the eyes of the Genoese agent, and indeed of most unprejudiced observers, Cromwell was the greatest power in the country. But the Council of State and what remained of Parliament were still the theoretical source of all authority. In the months during which Cromwell had been fighting Parliament's battles, Parliament had done very little to justify its existence. The Commons had made adultery a capital offence ; they had brought in the Navigation Act to undermine the Dutch carrying trade and had declared war on the United Provinces. But as for proceeding to the reform of the franchise in accordance with the principles laid down in the *Agreement of the People*, nothing seemed further from their thoughts.

Cromwell found the delay unpardonable. By his own account, he wished, after the Battle of Worcester, to retire like Fairfax into private life. Ludlow and Whitelocke give a different view of his behaviour. According to them, his conduct in the autumn and winter of 1651 betrayed a mind ambitious for power. In a discussion of the future settlement of the country, as Whitelocke long afterwards remembered, or said that he remembered, Cromwell had declared that they could not dispense with monarchical authority, significantly asking the question : " What if a man should take it upon him to be king ? "

Such a statement is not out of keeping either with Cromwell's views or with his expressed desire for retirement. The state in which he found the country after the Battle of Worcester justified him in postponing his leisure to a better time. Confident both of his own ability and of divine guidance, he was easily convinced that he had a duty to remain in office for some time longer. With his traditional political views, he might well have uttered the opinions attributed to him by Ludlow and Whitelocke, rather in some bewildered groping after a solution than with any idea of seizing the monarchical power himself.

His first constructive movement towards a settlement was to hurry an Act of Pardon and Oblivion through Parliament. While he was later to be a harsh judge of all those who sought to cause fresh disturbance in the country, he was genuinely anxious to reconcile the defeated party with the new Government, and to allow them as far as possible to have their share in the privileges of citizenship.

He was placed on several committees – on that for the reform of the legal system, for laws touching the relief of the poor and for the propagation

e Gospel. On this latter committee he dis-
ished himself at once by advocating the
t possible basis for toleration. But work on
committees meant little enough, when nothing
was done to give the country a new and stable
constitution or to carry out the provisions laid
down by the *Agreement of the People*, to which
Cromwell was himself in honour bound. He, and
with him his fellow-officers, soon began to find that
the sloth of Parliament was causing discontent in the
Army and unrest in the country. Meanwhile, the
Dutch war cost money, to raise which the lands
and goods of Royalists were still being confiscated.
In such circumstances Cromwell's Act of Oblivion,
passed in February, 1652, was likely to remain a
dead letter.

By August the patience of the Army was all but
exhausted. The Commons, purged as they had
been, were returning to their old customs. Fearing the Army and abhorring the idea of government by force of arms, they were intent on prolonging their own existence, so as to prevent the
re-organisation of England at the Army's will.

On August 12th, 1652, the Army officers presented a petition asking for a speedy consideration
of their own and the country's grievances. The
Commons, after some windy evasions, agreed to
appoint a Committee to confer with the officers
on public matters. This conference, which met in
October, produced a remedy in the form of a Bill
for the calling of a new Parliament and the
reform of the franchise. Under pressure, the
Commons agreed to set a limit to their present
assembly. They chose November, 1654, thus
allowing themselves a full two years. Meanwhile the *Agreement of the People* mouldered.

Cromwell was loth to precipitate yet another

crisis. He tried every other means of bringing
Parliament to reason first. It was over a year since
the Genoese agent had declared that he could do
anything he pleased, yet he petitioned the Commons and spoke at conferences mildly enough, as
if it had not lain in his hands to overturn Parliament in an instant. His respect for the constitution as he understood it, his fear of provoking
further trouble, restrained him through the eighteen
months which divided the Battle of Worcester from
the expulsion of the Long Parliament.

Chief among those who, in this last phase of the
conflict between Army and Parliament, attempted
to circumvent Cromwell in the Commons was Sir
Harry Vane. This ardent republican, who on the
eve of Marston Moor had appeared at York with
talk of deposing the King, was a man of more
acute and adventurous perceptions than Cromwell. He, like the Levellers but in a different
fashion, wished to see the King's execution followed to its logical conclusion. An intellectual
revolutionary, he had little understanding for the
immediate necessities of politics, but a clear conception of theory. Once Cromwell's admirer and
ally, he was now beginning to see in him – and
rightly as the event was to prove – that most
dangerous of all threats to the freedom of a people,
a potential military despot.

As Cromwell was to Vane an ambitious man
seeking autocratic power, so Vane was to Cromwell a tricky theorist, stealing the just gains of the
Army. Each was wrong about the other in theory,
and right in fact.

Vane thought it essential to prevent the Army
from assuming executive and judicial powers. If
the present House of Commons withdrew, what
could prevent the unimpeded rule of the soldiers ?

Cromwell would have answered this argument with the assertion that the Army most nearly represented the people, as things stood. Vane would have countered with the older theory that the Commons represented the people. Both would have been talking nonsense. Yet Cromwell, who desired the end of an insecure and transitional government in favour of some recognised authority, spoke on the whole a practical language which better expressed the needs of the country than the high-minded beliefs of Vane.

In the pursuance of his theories, Vane now tried to circumvent the Army by hastening through a Bill which should guarantee permanent sessions of Parliament. Although he was genuine enough in his desire to keep the Government in the control of a civil assembly, Cromwell could see nothing in this action but a wanton effort to rob Army and people of their due.

On April 20th, 1653, Cromwell went down to Westminster with a small troop of musketeers. Leaving them outside, he entered the House of Commons as though nothing were amiss, sat quietly down, and listened to a speech from Sir Harry Vane. When Vane had finished, he rose himself to speak. After placid and even courteous opening words, he gradually warmed into an impassioned attack on the slothful and dishonest methods of the Commons. Carried forward by the flood of his own oratory, he left his place and began to stamp up and down the floor of the House, glaring and gesticulating. " The Lord has done with you ! " he thundered out at the embarrassed assembly. As he came to his climax twenty or thirty musketeers filed into the House. Cromwell shouted to the Speaker to come down. Lenthall did not move and Harrison stepped forward with a grimly courteous offer to assist him. Lenthall then gathered up his robes and made as dignified an exit as he could. The rest of the members followed him out, leaving Cromwell stamping up and down in possession of the empty room. Swinging the mace off the table, " Take away this bauble," he shouted. And then, seeing the defeated Vane moving towards the door, burst out with vituperative scorn, " Sir Harry Vane ! Sir Harry Vane ! . . . May the Lord deliver me from Sir Harry Vane ! " He had already delivered himself.

The forcible expulsion of the Long Parliament left Cromwell sole master of the situation. In his own view, his power as commander-in-chief of the Army was boundless, but only provisional. He made no attempt to set up an immediate dictatorship. Instead, he clung forlornly to Parliamentary theory. His immediate action was to call another Parliament, and even this he did not by his own authority alone, but with the support of " my council of officers."

This Parliament which Cromwell opened in person on July 4th, 1653, was intended merely as a provisional assembly to work out the new Constitution of the country. It consisted of 140 members, not elected but nominated by Cromwell and his Council – a mockery of a Parliament, but the retention of the form was significant enough.

But so great had been the growth of free opinions in England during the last ten years that this nominated assembly proved even less suited to its purpose than its predecessor. If the percentage of old Parliament-men was small, the percentage of unorthodox and ardent newcomers, of Fifth Monarchy Men, Baptists and even

Quakers was correspondingly high. No sooner
were the members of the Little Parliament com-
fortably seated at Westminster than the more
violent among them took the bit between their
teeth, and Cromwell found that he had saved the
country from the deadening tactics of Vane only
to make it over to the breakneck rashness of
extremists. The most vocal section in the Little
Parliament were the members of the various individualist religious groups which had flourished
during the war. Projects, many of them admirable, for the reform of all existing institutions,
poured from the lips of the Army's nominees.
These ill-digested and insufficiently supported
plans culminated in the rejection of a Bill for
appointing and maintaining the clergy. Cromwell, like most men of his generation, feared that
if the State left the Church entirely to the caprice
of local worshippers, the service of God would
fall into utter decay. He wanted a wide basis for
liberty of conscience, but he had never contemplated the complete estrangement of Church and
State. Not so the Fifth Monarchy Men, the
Baptists, the Quakers. They believed that an
absolute severance of spiritual and secular matters
was the only road to salvation.

While Cromwell was still doubtful what next
to do, his own supporters in the House, and the
more moderate party, feeling that their colleagues
would soon tip the country over the edge into
dangerous anarchy, assembled very early one
morning, before the noisier extremists came, and
voted the dissolution of the gathering. They
resigned their power wholly into Cromwell's
hands, giving him, as he himself expressed it,
" power over the three nations, without bound or
limit set."

CHAPTER VII

OLIVER PROTECTOR : 1653–1655

The Instrument of Government – nature and extent of Cromwell's power – his Court and family – settlement of Scotland – settlement of Ireland – Cromwell's influence on religion – on education – on the arts and sciences – legal and administrative reforms – treaties with lesser Powers – First Protectorate Parliament – Royalist revolt – the Major-generals – opposition to Cromwell.

Two Parliaments having failed to make a Constitution for England, the Council of Officers took the matter into their own hands. The document, which was short for the weightiness of its matter, was called bluntly the *Instrument of Government*. Its chief architect seems to have been General John Lambert. By its provisions executive power was vested in a Protector, controlled and assisted by a Council of State. The legislative power, on the other hand, belonged to Parliament and Acts which it had passed became law with or without the Protector's consent – always supposing they contained nothing directly contrary to the Constitution.

During the intermission of Parliaments the Protector and his Council could issue ordinances which had the force of law until Parliament met, when they had to be submitted for its final sanction or annulment. In theory at least, Cromwell thus wielded a very limited power, and it is hard not to be amazed at the moderation or traditionalism – call it how one will – of those who, after two such experiences of Parliaments, still allowed to the Commons a controlling power in the State.

The concession was perhaps more theoretical than
actual for, as the Army officers well knew, the
last word in any political dispute lies with those
that bear the sword. On the other hand, supplies
were left in the control of Parliament, and the
principle which John Hampden had vindicated
nearly twenty years before was thus triumphantly
formulated in writing.

The composers of the new Constitution also met
the demand for franchise reform made in the
milder of the two *Agreements of the People* – not that
they extended the franchise itself, but they radically altered the decrepit borough system. They
disfranchised innumerable small boroughs and
filled up the places in Parliament by allotting a
far larger number of Members to the counties, the
numbers being graded according to size. This
arrangement was in reality nothing more than a
sensible acknowledgment of what had already
long been the case. The little boroughs returned
country gentlemen as often as not, the sons and
relations of the landowning gentry. The same
gentlemen now entered Parliament, as it were, in
their true colours, with no further pretence to
being essentially the deputies of towns rather than
of country districts. The Honourable Member for
East Retford, for instance, became one of the
Honourable Members for Nottingham. The only
important alteration was the creation of two new
boroughs, the rising towns of Leeds and Halifax.

On December 16th, 1653, Cromwell was installed as Protector at Westminster Abbey. It
was a simple ceremony, Cromwell himself being
dressed only in plain black velvet. For the
moment the country was calm and the new
Government to all outward appearances popular.
The Genoese agent, writing to inform his

masters that the Protector was an ally worth courting, recognised a political fact to which Cromwell still closed his eyes – that he, Oliver Cromwell, the individual, was the pillar on which alone the State rested.

What was the actuality and what the theory of Cromwell's position ? By the *Instrument of Government* he held his power under Parliament, and could govern autocratically only when Parliament was not sitting, all his actions being subject ultimately to the veto of that assembly. He was bound to consult them at not infrequent intervals because financial control was in their hands, and they were to make an even harsher use of this power than Cromwell anticipated. This, then, was the theory – not dictatorship, but a monarchy more severely limited by statute than that of the Stuarts.

Now the facts. As commander-in-chief of the Army, Cromwell had a greater power of physical coercion than any Stuart. But – and herein lay another, and this time unparliamentary, check on the Protector's power – how far could he rely on his Army ? The Levellers had been quelled, but among the most influential officers there were many whose views were far more emphatically republican than Cromwell's. He could not afford to offend these men, or at least not all of them, and unless he could trim his policy to please both them and Parliament, he would find himself deserted both by military force and economic assistance in his hour of need.

Cromwell acted throughout with the advice and assistance of a Council which he dominated but could not disregard. Here, too, there was latent opposition of another sort – from one ambitious officer at least, who sat at the Council table

Gc

meditating whether he was not a wiser man
than the Protector. This was the grave-faced
general whom Cromwell called "bottomless
Lambert" because he could not plumb his
secrets, or in happier moods, when he sought to
bury in a partly genuine affection his mistrust of
his clever colleague, his "dear Johnny."

One other check controlled Cromwell's
authority – his own theories. Events forced a
power upon him which he was nothing loth to
take, since he believed that he would use it well.
But he shrank from the outward signs of his
position, refused the name of king, compromising
with this new style of Protector, hedged his power
with restrictions which he would be forced in time
to disregard, and deliberately subjected himself
to the restraint of a written constitution. He was
no natural revolutionary and he valiantly disregarded what was revolutionary in his situation.
In his own mind he was always a "poor gentleman
that asks nothing better than to serve the public,"
or, as he even more graphically described it, a
constable paid to keep the peace in an unruly
parish. In his political theories he was for ever
groping his way back towards the normal. He
believed sincerely in Parliamentary government :
to have ceased to believe in it would have been to
admit that he had fought two wars for nothing,
that young Oliver and poor young Walton had
died in vain. Yet below all this brave pretence,
he realised the hopelessness of attempting a
permanent settlement. He could not, on that
account, abandon the principles for which he had
striven and on which he had once hoped that a
settlement might be made.

His attitude to personal liberty remained always
the same in theory. He held that "it was an

unjust and unwise jealousy to deprive a man of his natural liberty upon a supposition he may abuse it : when he doth abuse it, judge." Unhappily, Cromwell's subjects and Parliaments were all too much given to the abuse of their personal liberty, as he saw it. He was to be for ever judging.

Cromwell was not personally ambitious, or at least not inordinately so. Those who upbraid him with this vice misunderstand both the man and the period if they base their arguments on the position, lands and honours which he gained. He was certainly granted great possessions, for he owned six or seven palaces and kept a state at Whitehall as great as any in Europe. But could he have done less ? The modern taste for simplicity in dictators was foreign to the social outlook of that time. The ascetic indifference to honours of a Lenin would not much have impressed the seventeenth century, and would not have served to strengthen Cromwell's power. Disregard for social distinction had no place in his nature and was in fact unusual in his time. The determined example in the arduous flouting of the conventions set by the Levellers in politics, and by the Quakers in social life, met with extraordinarily little sympathy and even less admiration from contemporaries.

Cromwell speaking in the House of Commons in a badly cut home-spun suit was ridiculous : Cromwell fulfilling the duties of a sovereign in an ill-made suit would have been more than ridiculous. He would have been shocking. There is no humour in Sir Philip Warwick's grave account of the improvement in his manners and attire when he came to rule over England. The thing was absolutely necessary. Necessary, too, was the

formality of Whitehall, the grave investitures, the
obsequious courtesies before the throne, the bare
heads of men who had once been his fellow-
officers, and the introduction of " Your Highness "
as the correct form of address. Republicanism at
this time bore no necessary connection with a
lesser formality and respect for authority : the
Court of the Dutch Republic was famous as the
most formal in Europe.

The old mother, always in a flutter for her boy's
safety, and the elderly wife did their best in the
circumstances. They made it all faintly ridiculous. So also did the daughters, enormously and
frankly enjoying their role as princesses. But it
was not the assumption of regal formality which
struck malicious critics : rather it was the failure
to assume it easily. When the Protector asked for
an orange to squeeze over his roast mutton – his
favourite sauce – the Lady Protectress shouted
out that oranges were a groat a-piece and he must
do without : so the story. It is improbable that
Mrs. Cromwell so far forgot herself, but the
circulation of such tales is eloquent of the impres-
sion which she made, poor thrifty soul, after a life of
sparing and contriving, called suddenly to plod
heavy-footed in the halls where the trim French
Queen had danced.

Even for his children Cromwell showed very
little ambition. Only under strong persuasion did
he appoint his son Henry Lord Deputy of Ireland,
and he did not give Richard even that training in
politics which he should have had. His two elder
daughters were married before the war ended,
Elizabeth at sixteen to John Claypole, a Northamptonshire landowner, and Bridget to Henry
Ireton. For her second husband, in 1651,
Bridget took at her father's bidding another of his

lieutenants, Charles Fleetwood. Neither Henry
nor Richard made startlingly wealthy marriages,
and if the younger girls did better than their sisters
they did not do so well as contemporaries had
expected. Frances was given to the Yorkshire
peer, Lord Fauconberg, and Mary threw herself
with a determination that broke down her father's
objections into the arms of the Earl of Warwick's
heir. Cromwell clearly thought not so much of
founding a dynasty as of settling his children
respectably in case of untoward events after his
death. In this he was triumphantly successful :
not one of them but died in comfortable circumstances and on English soil. Even his long-
surviving wife found a peaceful home with her
son-in-law, the bluff and hearty Claypole, a man
of no apparent political conviction and singularly
un-Puritan habits.

At the time of his elevation to the Protectorate,
Cromwell was approaching fifty-five years of age,
which was not young for the seventeenth century.
In fact he was the oldest effective ruler in Europe.
The King of Spain and the Emperor were each
seven or eight years his junior, although both
considered themselves past the prime of life. The
Grand Pensionary of Holland, John de Witt, was
in the early thirties. Queen Christina of Sweden
was less than thirty, as also the prince who
succeeded her as Charles X. The nearest to
Cromwell in age was the chief Minister of the
French Crown, Cardinal Mazarin, and even he
was three years younger. Moreover, few men in
the seventeenth century held positions such as
Cromwell now occupied without passing through
years of practical political training. All the training Cromwell had had in the art of government
had been gained in a few sessions of Parliament

and in the exercise of his authority as a Justice
of the Peace in a quiet English county. His
civil government, like his soldiering, was to be
unorthodox.

The Protectorate began with eight months of
unimpeded rule by Cromwell and his Council of
State, during which time the new Government
more than justified its existence. Cromwell's
first care was for the unification of the three
kingdoms, an ambitious scheme which worked
comparatively well during his lifetime and fore-
shadowed developments only to be fully realised
two generations later. He decreed that both
Scotland and Ireland should send representatives
to Parliament at Westminster, Scotland being
ruled under his authority by General Monck,
Ireland first by his son-in-law, Fleetwood, and
later by his son, Henry Cromwell. His plans for
the internal government of Scotland were
genuinely enlightened : he swept away the feudal
jurisdictions, privileges and servitudes which had
for some time past seriously hampered the natural
development of the country, and encouraged
trade with England and foreign countries. His
measures, combined with the firm and intelligent
management of George Monck, restored peace
and prosperity to the land and brought its national
development gradually into line with the more
modern and less remote states of Europe.

Cromwell's Irish policy, on the other hand,
may be partly excused, but cannot be defended.
The country, a prey to chaotic civil war for more
than ten years, was bound to derive some immediate benefit if only from the re-establishment of
civil order. Unfortunately Cromwell's policy was
based on a total ignorance of Irish history, a
misunderstanding of and indignation at the

troubles which had preceded his rule, and a
fanatical determination to make an end of popery.
He had also an army to satisfy and a revenue to
raise. Here as elsewhere his policy was unorthodox, but this time only in the gigantic scope
of its ruthlessness. In the worst possible sense, it
was a bold policy – in theory, in execution and in
effect wholly bad – for Cromwell aimed at
nothing less than settling the Irish question once
and for all, by stamping out the Catholic Church
and penning the native population into the inland
parts of Connaught and Clare. Confined to these
districts, the original inhabitants of the island
would be cut off from the English settlers by the
bogs and the River Shannon, and from the rest of
the world by the sea. In theory the plan had a
kind of brutal genius : in fact it could not be
carried out. Irish landowners could be driven
out and repatriated forcibly in their allotted
counties, but no English settler would take over
land unless he could be certain of a peasantry to
work it for him. Thus in effect a subject race
came into being in the lands which Cromwell's
settlers and soldiers took from the native owners.

In all, Cromwell's confiscations affected more
than half the land in Ireland, 11 million acres :
of these 3 million were worthless bog and something over a million were granted back to the
Irish in Clare and Connaught. Cromwell thus
had about 6 million acres, a third part of the
habitable land in the country, to divide among
the settlers. About 6,000 landowners were totally
deprived of their possessions, and some 30,000
Irishmen became exiles, not counting those others
– whose number also ran into a few thousands –
whom Cromwell had transported to Barbados.
The immense upheaval, the political consequences

and individual injustices of this system can hardly be overestimated. It has been compared to the confiscation of Czech lands in Bohemia by Ferdinand II in 1621, a comparison which, while giving Cromwell the sanction of the political practice of his time, is not without modern significance. Neither the Czech nor the Irish question has yet been fully solved and the rancour of centuries festers on. Neither Cromwell nor Ferdinand created the problem, but each, thinking to cut the gangrene from the body politic, by a clumsy misuse of the surgeon's knife, mangled, but could neither kill nor cure.

At the end of the war Cromwell promised amnesty to all the Irish not actually concerned in murder. The interpretation of the word " murder " in a country which has long been in the anarchy of civil war may cover a wide field. We have a modern instance. Cromwell's ruling virtually condemned about 100,000 Irishmen to death – in a country of less than a million. Humanity and a blessed inefficiency relaxed the law, and not more than 200 were executed, while some at least of the victims were hardly to be regretted. Active co-operation with the Government was taken as the only criterion by which the right of a landowner to preserve his estates could be judged, a ruling which bore hard against minors, women and the unfit, whose quiescence in the revolt placed them by default among Cromwell's enemies. The Catholic faith was altogether prohibited and all priests expelled. Here too the banishment order was laxly carried out, and the actual execution of priests came to an end with the war itself. In some ways indeed the proscribed faith was little if at all worse off than under Stuart rule : proscription was at least no new thing. The concentration camps for priests on the Arran islands were more curious, as early examples of this method of dealing with the enemies of a government, than effective in extinguishing the living faith of the people.

In favour of Cromwell's Irish rule the best that can be said is that it was orderly after a long period of chaos, and that his two lieutenants, Fleetwood and Henry Cromwell, moderated what and where they could. Judged as an individual, Cromwell may be pardoned much, for he acted sincerely if mistakenly and felt that he was doing what was best for a depraved and misled people. Judged by the harsher standards of history, he did an ill service to England, and to Ireland irreparable wrong.

In England, meanwhile, Cromwell had not let the grass grow under his feet. He set up a central authority to appoint ministers for the Church and local committees to see that they did their duties efficiently, thus combining the best elements of the Anglican and Presbyterian organisation, while allowing wide latitude of doctrine throughout the country. His Church covered Independents, Baptists and Presbyterians, while beyond its bounds the sects flourished freely. Besides this he set a commission on foot for the propagation of the Gospel in Wales.

He brought the universities under State control by sending down selected persons to visit them and enquire into their teaching. These visitations did not, however, interfere greatly with the freedom of intellectual life nor lower its standards. On the whole Cromwell's influence on learning and the more serious arts was good : it is a notable fact that when Church lands were put up for sale those connected with educational endowments were specifically exempted. As might have been expected, Cromwell emphasised the political and religious aspects of education, but his Government can claim the honour of being the first which made definite, if rare and scanty, grants for the maintenance of schools and teachers. He contemplated the foundation of a new college at Oxford and of a northern university at Durham.

The sciences were not neglected. The Royal Society, founded so soon after the accession of Charles II, had its root in the numerous clubs and gatherings for the purpose of scientific enquiry which had grown up under Cromwell's rule. The Protector's name stands to this day next after that of William Laud on the marble tablet commemorating the benefactors of the Bodleian Library at Oxford, a graphic witness to the triumph of learning over political antagonisms.

Cromwell next issued a series of regulations against cock-fighting, duelling and swearing. This group, which appear to have been mainly actuated by religious motives, were different from the later ordinances against horse-racing and the measures to curtail the licensing of ale-houses. The latter appear to have been mainly police measures, intended to prevent the dangerous concourse of large crowds of people, among whom sedition might be discussed or riots break out. As far as his own tastes were concerned, Cromwell was not one of the extreme Puritan group in these matters. He was interested in the breeding of horses and there is no direct evidence that he felt any strong moral disapproval of racing. His son-in-law, Claypole, a keen promoter of all kinds of sport, indulged freely and frequently in the habit of betting.

One man could hardly have changed Merrie England, and certainly Cromwell would not have been that man. If he was sober in his habits, he was not austere ; he loved music – except in church – enjoyed a day's hawking and a game of bowls, and even, it seems, noticed and appreciated good food. Moreover, he was quite incapable of damping the spirits of his own family, let alone of all England. The gay clothes of his daughters and their frank predilection for dancing scandalised many of his followers. On the other hand, the Puritan outlook, strengthening since the Reformation, increased its hold over all sections of society, while Cromwell's police measures, by compelling the people to indulge in their sports secretly and as far as possible silently, may have been partly responsible for our national habit of taking our pleasures sadly. The alteration in the character of the English people was in reality a gradual process, in which the Commonwealth stands midway between the Reformation and the Wesleyan movement. Fifty years before Cromwell was born his compatriots had bidden their preliminary farewell to " rewards and fairies."

Nor did the arts suffer so much under the Protectorate as has sometimes been stated. A rule of five years could no more have converted an artistic into an inartistic people than it could have changed Merrie England into glum Great Britain. The war had brought the exceptional artistic activity of King Charles' reign to a sudden end. Van Dyck's pupils had been dispersed. The taste and inclination, not to mention the money, of the great collectors had gone. But in estimating the artistic achievement of the Commonwealth it is only fair to remember that the period which

preceded it was altogether exceptional. Gradually, as peace resumed its hold on the country, the
arts came back into a modified favour. Samuel
Cooper enjoyed a rising popularity. The Dutch-
man Lely steadily built up his practice as a portrait
painter. There was less native talent in this
respect, but such as it was Cromwell seems to have
encouraged it. William Faithorne, an engraver
of exceptional sensibility, after a short period of
exile, returned to London in 1650 ; he was able
to do good business for the next ten years remov-
ing the heads of eminent Royalists from his plates
and inserting eminent Parliament men. For his
seals and much of his coinage, Cromwell employed
Thomas Simon, an acknowledged master of this
minor art.

Domestic architecture and the more extravagant arts could hardly be expected to flourish in
a land exhausted by a long war. The masques
and ballets, the elaborate entertainments which
had delighted society for the past fifty years, were
at an end. The drama was temporarily proscribed, to satisfy the sterner elements among
Cromwell's supporters. All the same, in 1656
Cromwell recognised the need for some form of
innocent popular diversion in London and gave
Davenant permission to institute a modified form
of dramatic entertainment. The poet opened the
venture with a play about Spanish atrocities in the
West Indies, recently invaded by the English,
which combined instruction, political propaganda
and amusement in a way which irresistibly recalls
the methods of modern dictatorships.

Naturally enough, Cromwell was more interested in civil government than in the arts. He
appointed new judges and passed ordinances for
the relief of debtors and for the reduction of legal

charges to the poor. He was anxious to reform the Court of Chancery, but here his efforts failed because of the dogged opposition of the lawyers. Unlike the modern dictator in this as well as in other ways, Cromwell was never able to enforce his will against the solid opposition of any large section of the community, and he was not certain enough of his power even to attempt it.

He failed not merely with Chancery but with the criminal code, which he regarded as too harsh and would willingly have altered. He felt, for instance, that capital punishment was too frequently inflicted. His views were typical of his practical, generous, yet illogical approach to legal subjects. He would gladly have spared the petty thief, but he was willing, if need be, to fly in the face of English tradition and to refuse traitors the right of trial by jury, when he thought that he might not secure a conviction. In 1654 Gerard and Vowell were denied the privilege of a jury when they were condemned to death for a plot against his life, and the Royalist Mordaunt appealed in vain for a jury four years later. Nevertheless, if Cromwell was prepared in an emergency to override even the scanty provisions made by English law for the protection of the accused, he genuinely desired more constructive and humane legislation. His failure to achieve anything in this direction is but another proof of the cavalier fashion in which Parliament treated his wishes, and of his own unwillingness to act on his unsupported authority. His Government, while it had few of the faults, had equally none of the virtues of the modern dictatorship.

He was more fortunate in his efforts towards administrative reform. He inherited from the Long Parliament an admirable Secretary of State

in John Thurloe. This exceptionally gifted man
was able to draw the threads of administration
together into his hands and to train an efficient
staff. The tradition which ascribes the formation
of the British Civil Service to Cromwell is basically
sound. Half-way through his reign we find the
rapacious Clerks of the Privy Seal and Signet
loudly lamenting that their fees and perquisites
have disappeared and imploring the Protector to
guarantee them instead a reasonable salary. It is
the dawn of a great reformation.

John Thurloe's other great achievement was the
creation of a startlingly efficient secret service, of
inestimable help to the Protector in gauging the
feelings of his own country and in directing his
foreign policy. For his Latin Secretary Cromwell
employed John Milton, who was assisted in his
office by yet another poet, Andrew Marvell.

Whether it was a chance, or whether it was
something in Cromwell's personality, or else the
harrow of the wars which, cleaving the English
earth, had thrown up so much talent, Cromwell,
unlike King Charles, found on all sides the men
he needed – Monck for Scotland, Thurloe for the
administration, Milton for foreign affairs, Blake
for the Navy. A team such as few rulers have
had at their command.

In foreign affairs the brief reign which was to
be so aggressively glorious opened with a more
sober and pacific policy. War with the United
Provinces, beginning in 1652, had for some
months past grievously strained the resources of
the Government. Cromwell's first act was to
bring this disgraceful commerical squabble to an
end. He has been criticised for throwing away
the gains of a hard-fought war by an indifferent
peace, but the terms of the treaty do not justify

the complaint. England gained every tangible advantage for which she had fought. Henceforward the Dutch guaranteed the security of her commerce in the East Indies, agreed to make good the losses previously suffered by English merchants, conceded the supremacy of the English flag in the Narrow Seas and swore to exclude the House of Orange, close kin to the House of Stuart, for ever from their government.

At the same time, in the spring of 1654, Cromwell signed favourable commercial treaties with Portugal and Sweden, and a few months later came to an agreement with Denmark by which the Sound was thrown open to English shipping. Thus in a few months he had laid the bases of a foreign policy reminiscent of that of Queen Elizabeth – a fundamentally peaceful policy of alliances with the lesser Powers, founded on community of commercial and sometimes even of religious outlook.

With these achievements already behind him, Cromwell opened his first Parliament on September 3rd, 1654, a significant anniversary. The failure of the Long and the Little Parliaments to provide England with a constitution might be regarded as inevitable in the circumstances ; that of the first Protectorate Parliament to endorse the provisions of the *Instrument of Government* or to meet the problems of the State was one of the hardest blows that Cromwell had to sustain. In a speech full of hope, he placed the ratification of his powers and the settlement of England in their hands. " Gentlemen," he began, " you are met here on the greatest occasion that, I believe, England ever saw : having upon your shoulders the interests of three great nations." He ended by urging them " to a sweet gracious and holy understanding of one another and of your business." All in vain.

Even a cursory perusal of the names of those who filled the House of Commons during the whole period of the wars and Commonwealth reveals the fact that the ruling class was too small to allow of any complete alteration in the personnel of Parliaments. The composition of the House to which Cromwell made his appeal was only in part different from that of its two predecessors. Half of its members – the most experienced and vocal half – had sat in Parliament before and were well acquainted with all the tricks whereby the power of the House of Commons could be asserted and maintained.

A man did not need to be a republican to feel that the supremacy of Parliament was the keystone of the Constitution. For what other principle had the war been fought? Nevertheless, it was the republicans from whom Cromwell had most to fear and from these that the initial onslaught on the *Instrument of Government* came. In order to prevent the complete stoppage of political life while Parliament tore up the Constitution, Cromwell very soon intervened, insisting that the members must at least agree to accept as a basis for discussion the Constitution which the Army officers had drawn up for them. His plan did not do much to expedite the political business of the country, for although it led to the withdrawal of the extreme republican element from the House, it did not prevent those who remained from battering the *Instrument* to pieces, clause by clause. The old struggle between civil and military authority had begun again in a new form, typified by the claim of the Commons to have the ultimate control of the Army.

Calculating that Cromwell would not dare to dissolve them until they had granted supplies, for he had no legal right to raise money without them, the Commons imagined that they were safe. They reckoned without the Protector. He let them sit to the limit of the time prescribed for Parliaments by the *Instrument of Government* – five months, and he made them lunar, not calendar, months ! – and then dissolved them. It is easy to understand what prompted his action : his Government, stable during the period of his absolute ascendancy, was gravely shaken by the behaviour of his Parliament. Criticism, by revealing that Cromwell had not very much more support among the ruling class than King Charles had had, encouraged rebellion against him, both on the Right and on the Left. The Royalists believed that there was a chance for their King, the Levellers for their republic.

Kept informed by an efficient spy-service, the work of the careful Thurloe, Cromwell knew the gravity of the situation and saw in the resumption of personal control the only way to save the nation from disaster. " The people will prefer their safety to their passions and their real security to forms," he stormed, showing a curious lack of appreciation of his countrymen's outlook. Most dangerous of all, he had now openly taken the formula of *salus populi suprema lex* for his own.

Judged by standards of political expediency, he had been right to dissolve Parliament. The storm burst immediately afterwards and Cromwell was better able to guide the ship of State through it alone than with the Commons officiously snatching at the wheel. Parliament was dissolved on January 22nd, 1655. In the early spring the Levellers began to raise their heads

Hc

once more. Cromwell did what he could to conciliate such of them as did not directly threaten his Government. After an interview with George Fox, he allowed the Quaker movement to gather momentum unmolested. Not from the Quakers but from the Anabaptists and Fifth Monarchy Men, among them Cromwell's old companion-in-arms, Thomas Harrison, came the real danger. Their preachers had to be restrained, their leaders arrested.

More serious still was the Royalist revolt in Wiltshire, which broke out in March under the leadership of John Penruddock. Immediate and widespread arrests of Royalists, followed by confiscations and civil penalties, brought the trembling country to heel. The Genoese agent estimated that the Protector had deprived four-fifths of the ruling class of their privileges. The exaggeration was significant in so far as it reflected the fear and amazement of the land.

Unsupplied by Parliament Cromwell naturally used the revolt to raise more money for his Government. Apart from the new confiscations, he imposed a capital levy of a tenth, a " decimation," on the Royalists, out of which he defrayed the cost of a new form of military rule imposed on the country. He divided England into districts, each to be controlled by a Major-general with almost unlimited authority. These officers were to see to the execution of Government ordinances, to keep a register of the inhabitants of their districts and to record their comings and goings, and, strange confusion of police and moral measures, were to " promote godliness and virtue " by all the means in their power. They had authority to break up public meetings, to close ale-houses and to search dwellings.

The rule of the Major-generals marks the high-tide of Cromwell's dictatorial power. England was now under a military despotism which interfered in every sphere of private life. Individual freedom, in political matters at least, had seldom been at a lower ebb – certainly not for the last hundred years. Cromwell had for the time being completely abandoned his policy of conciliation. Furthermore, he was undermining public confidence and self-respect by a system of spies and intelligencers such as has never been seen in England since. His rule by the summer of 1655 had developed many of the most repulsive characteristics of tyranny.

There is, however, a distinction between a tyranny which is an end in itself and one which is but a means to another end. Even at the worst moments, Cromwell never wholly lost sight of this distinction. Naturally bad-tempered, and embittered now by opposition and disappointment, he would occasionally burst forth with statements of a naked and brutal violence, declaring that the people were unfit to know their own good and that the sword alone was the best means of government. But his policy in the long run belied his moments of rapid anger. He tightened his control over the rebellious land only to save it from itself, and he fully intended when occasion arose to relax that hold again. His autocracy did not increase in severity as time went on. After those bad months in 1655 it gradually lessened.

Driven by monarchical revolt to abandon his policy of conciliation, Cromwell was driven by republican revolt to curtail his policy of toleration. Plots and risings among Levellers and Anabaptists forced him to limit his previous concessions and arrest the leaders of the sects.

Nor were revolts to the Left and Right all that he had to meet. Under the weight of his increasing absolutism, the Centre began to give. Two judges, Whitelocke and Widdrington, resigned as a protest against his meddling with Chancery. Two others, Newdigate and Thorpe, refused to carry out his policy against Royalist rebels in the north. When a merchant named Cony refused to pay his Customs dues, denying the validity of the new Constitution, Cromwell called upon Lord Chief Justice Rolle to defend the legality of the dues, and Rolle incontinently resigned his office.

Unable to pacify monarchists or republicans, deserted by the gentry, the merchants and the bench, accused of personal ambition by men who had once been his friends, Cromwell could no longer be blind to the horror of his situation. So long as he had the loyalty of the Army, so long as he had his efficient and obedient servants, his Government was in itself secure. But it was a travesty of any government that he might have wished to set up. It rested on force, it had failed to secure the liberties for which he himself had fought, and it had no future beyond his death. Bitterly he wrote to his son-in-law, Fleetwood, in that cruel summer of 1655 : " The wretched jealousies that are amongst us and the spirit of calumny turn all into gall and wormwood."

CHAPTER VIII

FOREIGN POLICY : 1655–1658

Cromwell's outlook – plans for a Protestant league – the Vaudois
– rivalry of Denmark and Sweden – Blake in the Mediterranean – breach with Spain – Santo Domingo and Jamaica
– alliance with France – Santa Cruz – Battle of the Dunes –
cession of Dunkirk – appreciation of Cromwell's policy.

CONSTITUTIONALLY Cromwell's Government had
failed. The most that can be said for it was that
it gave the country peace, security and time to
recover from the war. It had no permanent
value.

Barren as this strong Government was to prove,
its success in European politics while it lasted was
miraculous. Much has been said both for and
against Cromwell's foreign policy. One fact,
however, cannot be disregarded : whatever
England may have lost later by Cromwell's
actions, she regained at the time both her prestige
abroad and her own self-respect.

Cromwell was not likely to be an outstanding
diplomatist. He had even less training in this
most expert craft than in civil and military affairs :
nor is the soldier's or the politician's genius the
same as that of the diplomatist. He came to
power with little more than the average country
gentleman's knowledge of European politics, and
the inept intervention of Parliament in foreign
affairs in the early part of the century had shown
how little that knowledge was. Religion was the
driving force of Cromwell's life, and so, inevitably,
of his foreign policy. But religion had ceased to
be the driving force of European politics about

twenty years before Cromwell became Protector. The Thirty Years' War had made an end of it. National egoism and dynastic ambition, closely interwoven, now set the pace.

Bred in those years of national retrogression which followed the unnatural and too early flowering of the Elizabethan Age, Cromwell could hardly avoid that sense of impotent resentment which had marked the attitude of Englishmen to foreign politics in King James' reign. His mind never expanded beyond the views expressed by a Sir John Eliot in the later Parliaments of King James, when it had become apparent to a shocked and ignorant gentry that the government under which they lived neither could nor would rescue Protestant Czechs and Protestant Germans from the onslaught of the Austrian and the Spaniard. Cromwell's foreign policy was therefore dominated in part by religion and in part by the desire to wipe out what most of his contemporaries had regarded as a national disgrace. The fact that the time for action was now thirty years gone by did not occur to him.

If England had ever intended to challenge Spain seriously, she should have done so in the early 1620's. A generation too late, when Spain was already beaten, Cromwell entered a war which was, to all intents and purposes, already over. His policy was not only an anachronism ; it was strongly disapproved of by the growing mercantile element in the country, who were perfectly aware by this time that Catholic Spain was no longer a danger and Protestant Holland was. But the merchant vote controlled neither Parliament nor the Council, and Cromwell had his way.

The war had brought men of action to the front : the subsequent efforts of Prince Rupert to fight the

King's cause from the sea had led to a renewed interest in the Navy, already much improved under Charles I, and had awakened the English to a sense of their ability and vocation as seamen. The Dutch war had confirmed this. Above all, there was Robert Blake, whose genius and personality were to give to a good Navy a commander at last worthy of it.

The strength of the English Army and Navy had caused some anxiety abroad even before Cromwell became Protector, and when the Government was stabilised in the hands of a man known to be ruthless, resolute and a great soldier, these fears bore fruit in an increased respect. Cromwell, bringing to foreign policy the same conviction of heavenly guidance that he had brought to civil government, took this for a sign of God's grace. He was in the course of five years to imbue English foreign relations with that strong moral tone which is still with us. Not for nothing was it at this time that Milton, unconscious of absurdity, perpetrated his statement about God and his Englishmen.

From the moral point of view, Cromwell wanted an alliance of the Protestant against the Catholic Powers. From the point of view of English prestige, he wanted rights of trade and colonisation and was determined to show that England could hold her own, not merely in the Narrow Seas, but in the Mediterranean. From the commercial and strategic viewpoint he wanted foothold on the further side of the Channel to ensure safety for English merchants and shipping. There were too many elements in this policy for it to be universally consistent with itself.

Cromwell's Protestant alliance failed because he had not allowed for the antagonisms of the other

Protestant Powers. In the summer of 1655 a wave of indignation swept the Protestant countries at the savage attack made by the Duke of Savoy on their co-religionists, the Vaudois. Cromwell seized the opportunity to promote his general alliance. His moral indignation was genuine : it would hardly have been so effective otherwise. He himself headed the public subscription for the oppressed with a gift of £2,000. Meanwhile, Blake appeared threateningly in the Mediterranean. Fortunately for the Vaudois and not altogether fortunately for Cromwell, Mazarin promptly scotched the Protestant alliance by taking the case into his own hands and sharply calling the Duke of Savoy to order. The cause for united action being thus removed, the projected alliance failed to materialise.

Other reasons, too, prevented the successful formation of such a league. Cromwell was only temporarily successful in making peace between Sweden and Denmark. Before the end of his brief reign the two northern kingdoms were once again at each other's throats, and this time the two other northern Protestant Powers took sides, Brandenburg and the United Provinces both supporting Denmark. Cromwell, on the contrary, allied himself with Sweden, gaining what commercial advantage he could from the breakdown of his religious foreign policy, by bargaining to have Elsinore and Kronborg when the Danish King had been beaten.

The second part of Cromwell's foreign policy, the development of English prestige through sea-power, was triumphantly carried out thanks to the genius of Blake. In the spring of 1655 he entered the Mediterranean and forced the Dey of Algiers to release the English prisoners in his galleys.

Certain Dutch slaves, too, who entreated the help
of those who but a year before had been their
enemies, were freed by ransom raised by subscription among Blake's seamen. It is a moving story
worthy of record, yet as an antidote to national
complacency it is well to remember that only a
short while before the Genoese Government was
complaining in London of an English pirate who
raided the Italian coast for slaves to sell to the
Turks. In any case, Blake's voyage was not
undertaken for purely humanitarian motives, but
rather to demonstrate English sea-power in the
Mediterranean, and more particularly to the
Spaniard.

In the New Year of 1655 another naval expedition had set out, to challenge Spain, this time in
the West Indies. Here the rivalry between Spaniard and Englishman was ready to explode into
war. The Spaniards resented English interference in a part of the world which they had
themselves discovered and to which a Papal
charter gave them an exclusive right. They set
on English merchant ships in the Caribbean Sea
and handed over the crews to the Inquisition as
heretics. As Cromwell not unreasonably said, to
justify sending his warships to the Indies, either
there was peace among the islands or there was
not. If there was not, then the Spaniards were to
blame.

The two admirals sent to the West Indies, Penn
and Venables, had not Blake's genius. Their
attack on Santo Domingo, a lamentable failure in
itself, precipitated an open war with Spain for
which Cromwell was hardly prepared. The
seizure of the then barren island of Jamaica did
not, to his mind, in the least outweigh the disgraceful mismanagement of the attack on Santo

Domingo, and the immediate prospect of European repercussions from the failure of the *coup* was far more disturbing than the possession of an island, later to be a valuable part of the West Indian Empire, was gratifying. Penn and Venables were placed under arrest.

When the attack on his property was reported in Spain, the King at once sent an ambassador extraordinary to Cromwell to discuss a settlement. If Philip IV to some extent underestimated England's new power, he was nevertheless anxious if he could to avoid a clash with yet another enemy. He had been at war with France for more than twenty years, and although he did his best to undermine his enemies by subsidising rebels within their own country, the outcome of the conflict was no longer in serious doubt. But Philip's government was as fanatical as Cromwell's, and when the Protector asked for trading rights for his subjects in the West Indies, together with permission for English merchants to practise their religion unmolested, he met with an extravagant refusal. It was, said the Spanish Ambassador, as though Cromwell had asked for his master's two eyes.

Cromwell was later, when speaking before Parliament, to make much of this religious aspect of the matter. Yet English trading interests in the Indies, rather than the religion of English seamen, was the cause for which he had risked challenging Spain. The attack on Santo Domingo was perhaps not wholly unprovoked aggression, but it was aggression none the less, and it was conceived, as most aggression is conceived, in highly righteous terms. Later there was to be much talk of protecting the natives from Spanish oppression. One of Cromwell's sea-captains, writing to a

friend before the expedition sailed, asked for
" your prayers that we may be sent out with a
blessing and be a blessing where we go." An
attack on the land of another people was en-
visaged as a crusade. The conception is a little
too familiar to ring altogether pleasantly in
modern ears.

The ill-fortune of the Spanish war forced
Cromwell to accept the French alliance. Mazarin
was glad to have English help in order to increase
his already excellent chances of victory in the
Spanish war which, after twenty years, he was
conducting to a conclusion. Cromwell's agreement to this new friendship has been much
attacked. His assistance certainly ensured Mazarin's victory, vitiated his own scheme for a united
Protestant front and did much to create the huge
power of France, the bogy of the coming generation. But in the circumstances it is hard to see
what else he could have done. The failure at
Santo Domingo forced him to find European
allies, and Mazarin's quick intervention in the
Vaudois problem wrecked the Protestant alliance
which he had contemplated. In the hour of his
greatest need, no other ally save France could
be found.

Even in these straits Cromwell was able, not
indeed at his initial treaty, but at the signing of
a second offensive and defensive alliance in
March, 1657, to gain commercial advantages even
if he compromised his moral position. As the
price of military help in Flanders he demanded
the session of Mardyke and Dunkirk. From this it
has been inferred, not without justification, that
the French alliance marked not so much the
abandonment of Cromwell's religious foreign
policy as the preliminary move in an attack which

he did not live to carry out on England's greatest commercial rival – the United Provinces.

Shortly after the second French treaty, Blake redeemed the catastrophe of Santo Domingo by burning and looting the Spanish treasure fleet in the harbour of Santa Cruz. In the following summer French and English troops broke the Spaniards at the Battle of the Dunes and nine days later Dunkirk was handed over to the English Government. Mardyke had been ceded some months before. By the midsummer of 1658 Cromwell had given England a position in European affairs more impressive than any she had yet held.

Not Henry VIII, not Elizabeth, had achieved such greatness for their country. True that the position was untenable, based on a nation which had neither the resources nor the man-power to maintain it and was already heavily burdened with debt. True that England would inevitably drop from that height to an humiliating subservience, and that the decline was implicit in the situation of 1658. True that the moral, national and commercial elements of Cromwell's policy were in conflict one with another. In foreign affairs as in English, he was compelled by circumstances to abandon his original plan and make shift to do what he could with the fragments left to him.

Yet Cromwell, like Elizabeth, added something vital to the historic memory of his people and in so doing set the tone for the future of British policy. The Lord who had guided his hand when he fought in England did not forsake him abroad. The Lord who inspired Cromwell's policy became the Lord who inspired the Empire. An ingenuous and frank self-righteousness, mingled with a keen sense of commercial advantage, was Cromwell's legacy to English policy. It has suffered eclipses : it has been sometimes more frankly stated than at others, but always it returns and always it is essentially the same as when Cromwell, speaking to the Parliament of 1656, declared in one breath that God had made the Spaniard our natural enemy and in the next that " the ground of necessity, for justifying men's actions, is above all considerations of instituted law." His officers prayed and wrought as he did. " All that look towards Zion should hold Christian communion – we have all the guns aboard," wrote one. The guns were not to defend Zion. They were to blast the rival trader.

CHAPTER IX

THE END : 1656–1658

Financial difficulties – Cromwell opens the Second Protectorate Parliament – *The Humble Petition and Advice* – Second Session of Parliament – Cromwell and religion – Cromwell and the administration – family affairs – death of Lady Claypole – Cromwell's illness and death – his family – his political beliefs – his achievement.

AFTER the failure of his first Parliament, Cromwell had governed unaided for about eighteen months. In the autumn of 1656 pressing financial need forced him once again to call the Commons. He had calculated wrongly that the Spanish war would pay for itself. His policy, whatever later benefits it conferred on English commerce, was not a merchant's policy : it was a true reflection of the rash spirit of the Elizabethan Age, adventurous, risky and extravagant – particularly the latter. By modern standards, Cromwell's annual budgets of between 2 and 3 million pounds seem ridiculously small, nor were they very large by contemporary European reckoning. Financiers like Wallenstein had dealt in far larger sums. But English public finance was hampered by an outworn and inadequate system of taxation, unequal to the widening needs of the country. Small as Cromwell's budgets were, they were far larger than anything hitherto contemplated by English rulers. Nor was this accounted for by any marked improvement in the social services. Exclusive of Cromwell's household, on which he spent £50,000 – £20,000 less than the impoverished Charles I – the Civil List accounted for a sum

of less than £200,000, while in 1654, a year of
peace, the Army and Navy between them
swallowed 2½ millions. Cromwell was thus
spending more than ten times as much on arma-
ments and potential warfare than on everything
else combined, a disproportion only in part
accounted for by the fact that the social services
were still in the main paid for locally.

This would have been all very well if there had
been means for raising the money. But there were
none. The Long Parliament, wise in its own
generation, had avoided extravagance and had
died, so to speak, solvent. As the years passed the
deficit piled up. Customs and excise, the monthly
assessments imposed in time of war and maintained afterwards, semi-forced loans, sale and
confiscation of goods, Spanish prizes – all were not
enough to meet the mounting bills. Cromwell,
who believed in his policy, would have taxed
without Parliament in order to carry it out ; but
his power was never so certain that he could afford
to show this red rag to the English bull. He had
had trouble enough when he raised the Customs
dues without consent.

As the years went on, the credit of his Government sank at home. Two City merchants, both
once Members of Parliament and men of great
wealth, Vassell and Avery, were shut up in
debtor's prisons because they had been unable to
redeem the great sums they had advanced to the
Government. This was a poor encouragement to
other City men. Another appeal to the Commons
seemed the only way and in September, 1656,
Cromwell opened his second Parliament.

The merits of his opening speech were easier to
judge in the nineteenth century when, as Carlyle
declared, the " cursory modern Englishman "

would find its matter strange enough to have difficulty in reading it through. The cursory modern Englishman of to-day knows the like of that speech so well that he can no longer close his eyes and ears to it. He has heard it shrieked over the wireless, he has read it, point by point, in the greyish print of the stop-press columns. There is nothing strange to us, as there was to Carlyle, in this terrific outpouring of belief in a mission. Diction alters and " race " may take the place of " God." Cromwell's headlong utterance has little in common with the more skilful effects to which we have grown accustomed. But the structure of the speech has not altered. The Protector demanded the rights, the preservation, the natural development of a people of whose divine mission and natural superiority he had no doubt, of a people encircled by vicious and jealous enemies intent on their destruction. Next he elucidated, with all the passion that we expect to-day – but, it must be admitted, with less logic : " Why, truly, your great enemy is the Spaniard. He is a natural enemy. He is naturally so ; he is naturally so throughout " – then, realising the weakness of this, he added with a rush – " by reason of that enmity that is in him against whatsoever is of God." That the English were " of God " had already been demonstrated. And then followed that great mass of undigested history tied up with references to recent " incidents," gathering momentum as the words rolled on into a terrific and almost mystical outburst of wrath against the foe. " Therefore I say that your danger is from the Common Enemy abroad ; who is the head of the Papal interest, the head of the Anti-Christian interest." He tacked and turned in his speech, indicted the recalcitrant and

rebellious within the land, dwelt on the dire need
of the Treasury and swung out again into a
rhetorical appeal to Parliament to stand by him
because he was one with the nation, " by the
Voice of the People the Supreme Magistrate,"
because they were " knit together in one bond, to
promote the glory of God against the Common
Enemy." And so on.

To the modern ear this outburst is one of the
saddest things in English history. Its lack of
coherence, its blunt, bludgeoning, discursive
weaknesses, its threatening, destructive, blustering
approach, all betray that the worst elements of
power were affecting Cromwell's brain. It was
not the speech of an absolutely sane man. It was,
however, a speech which momentarily at least
was calculated to please a people delighted with
their recent successes and flattered to find themselves set up as the mentors of the world. Born of
the worst and most unreasoning elements in
Cromwell, it appealed to the worst and most
unreasoning elements in those whom he governed.
It marks the lowest point in Cromwell's moral
decline and it speaks much for the true greatness
of his character that he was ever again able to
rise out of this mire of rhetoric and self-deception.

The success of Cromwell's Government abroad,
the re-establishment of peace at home, had
increased his popularity. But he took no chances,
for he had arranged that members whose views
were known to be dangerous should be prevented
from taking their seats. About 100 were turned
back at the very door of the House. Those who
remained did not appear to resent this interference with their privileges and on the face of it
it seemed that Cromwell was for the first time to
have a manageable Parliament. Yet even under

Ia

the surface of this assembly the old hatred between civil and military authority governed the course of debate. But this time Cromwell's popularity itself was to be used as a tool against the Army.

Parliament raised its voice loudly against the Major-generals. In place of this military rule, it wished to set up a new civil authority, a monarchy under Cromwell. This was the last turn in the long game played out between Parliament and Army, in which so far Parliament had been defeated. Much depended on what Cromwell would do, and Cromwell, able soldier as he was, refused to make a move until he saw how the land lay.

The session dragged on, public business being suddenly held up by one of those incidents which repeatedly in the seventeenth century would draw off the attention of the Commons even from the most important constitutional matters. James Naylor, a Quaker, in a period of temporary aberration, had allowed his followers to hail him as Christ. Horrified by this appalling blasphemy, Parliament took the case out of the hands of the civil courts and excelled themselves in devising a punishment fit for the abominable crime. Cromwell for political reasons challenged their power to sit in judgment on the culprit, and for genuinely humane reasons appealed for milder treatment. Neither action had any effect.

Meanwhile, the fantastic plot of Miles Sindercombe against the Protector's life was revealed at about Christmas-time and a genuine revulsion of feeling in Cromwell's favour culminated in a vote of £400,000 for the Spanish war. The knowledge that supplies were at last to be given probably decided Cromwell to sacrifice the Army to Parliament for the time being. In January, 1657,

Claypole, speaking as his mouthpiece, brought in the Bill for abolishing the Major-generals.

But constitutional reform hung fire, Cromwell still hesitating to offend the Army leaders by accepting the Crown which the Commons were ready to offer him. On March 31st Parliament presented him with its *Humble Petition and Advice* offering to make him constitutional King. Cromwell, after a month's politic hesitation, definitely refused the Crown on May 7th. After that the *Humble Petition and Advice* lost much of its point. The document which procured the Protector's sanction on May 25th was comparatively insignificant. Cromwell was given power to nominate his successor, and a month later he was again installed as Lord Protector under the new Constitution, with greater pomp than before. He himself signalised his alliance with Parliament at the Army's expense by dismissing John Lambert, whose rivalry on the Council was irksome if not actually suspect.

After the summer recess Parliament met again in January, 1658. In the meantime Cromwell had selected a number of men, some of them Members of Parliament, to form the Upper, or " Other," House, which was the only other significant innovation in the new Constitution. Thus, when Parliament met, the Commons were denuded of his ablest supporters. Worse still, the 100 excluded members had been quietly allowed to resume their seats under the new Constitution. Cromwell was now to find that the civil authority had not learnt better manners from its long suppression. Grievances, the Commons began aggressively, must be redressed before they could grant any more supplies. It seemed that the sum voted in the summer had already been engulfed in the wars. This placed them in a very strong position. The next move of the Lower House was to initiate an acrimonious argument with Cromwell's " Lords " as to whether or not they really were " Lords."

Cromwell felt that there was nothing to be gained by prolonging this kind of session. Thirty years' experience of Parliaments had taught him exactly what it would lead to. Rumours of plots, unearthed by the indefatigable Thurloe, gave him his excuse to be rid of the assembly, supply or no. If he had to call Parliament again he would probably be luckier, and he could hardly be less lucky, with its personnel, if he started with a fresh election. Fifteen days after opening the session, on February 4th, 1658, Cromwell came down to the House in a towering passion and for the third time in five years forcibly dissolved the representatives of the people. " Let God be judge between you and me ! " he stormed, the last words of his which were to ring out in an assembled Parliament.

Cromwell had achieved nothing, either through Parliament or in the constitutional sphere. He had not solved the problems for which the war had been fought, and after the final dissolution of his second Parliament he seems to have abandoned all hope of doing so. After the last abortive plots against him, he used the revulsion of feeling in his favour to work once again for the appeasement of all sections of the community : but a permanent constitutional settlement was further off than ever before.

Not in this sphere is to be found the greatness of Cromwell's civil government. Yet it would be unfair to say that because he failed to solve the problems for which the war had been fought, he

failed altogether. He gave England five years of
security and comparative prosperity after long
travail : he made possible by his measured and
unvindictive, if stern, handling of the Royalists a
calm and almost bloodless return to the monarchy.
This latter was naturally not his intention, but
this should not derogate from his merit in causing
it. And again, in spite of the political pressure
which prevented his measures from taking effect,
he established for the imitation of future ages a
standard of toleration. He divorced religion from
its territorial basis, the *cujus regio ejus religio* principle which had fettered it for so long. Although
he did not allow Catholic worship, he did not,
as the Anglican government had done, penalise
Catholics for not attending the religious worship
authorised by the State. Even this was an
advance. In the main he recognised the right of
every man to possess his soul in freedom, so long
as his belief did not lead to flagrantly anti-social
conduct. He loathed the necessity of persecution,
and that for his time and age was broad enough.
His generous encouragement of the Quakers, in
some ways the most extreme, as they were
also the most constructive, of the new sectaries,
was much to his credit. So also was his persistent
defence of James Naylor; it is an eloquent com-
ment on Cromwell's actual subjection to Parliament during its sessions that he was able to help
him so little.

Interesting too, at this time, was Cromwell's
project for giving the Jews a home in England.
It broke down on the opposition of the City, and
the Protector had to rest contented with giving
them liberty to enter and live in the country and
to set up their synagogues.

For his zealous reform of administration, for the

honesty and efficiency of his rule, the country should have been truly grateful. Marred as were the five years of his government by the decimation of the Cavaliers, by the proscription and arrests of Levellers, Anabaptists, Fifth Monarchy Men, by the spy system and the rule of the Major-generals, yet taken as a whole they were good years for England – years of rest and recovery.

Finance was the weak part of Cromwell's administration, as it was of most European administrations at that time. He was to leave a debt of 2 million pounds, which may have had something, though not everything, to do with the fall of his son. This debt was nearly twice as large as that left by James I, but Cromwell had more to show for it. His Government, like that of Charles I, had aimed high ; he had wanted, although he had not succeeded in getting, better education for the people and better care for the poor. The social conscience was awake and at work even if the seventeenth-century philanthropist cared disproportionately more for the soul than the body : even if, among a tight-fisted merchant class, the belief that poverty was in itself a crime was gradually taking root. In actual achievements Cromwell's government had as little to show for its aspirations as that of Charles I. But Cromwell had done something which Charles I had not ; he had established a new tradition. Thurloe laid the strong foundation of English administrative tradition and managed to co-ordinate the branches of the administration as the happy-go-lucky secretaries of King Charles had never done.

There was, of course, no revolutionary change, and the development grew out of a need for efficiency, rather than from a constructive plan. In no sphere did Cromwell show originality, and indeed in finance his natural conservatism led him not only to restore the Exchequer in 1654, but to stereotype the questionable fiscal methods of his predecessors rather than to evolve any new and all-embracing scheme. A more original thinker could perhaps have built up a real autocracy, but Cromwell stumbled on, differing in nothing from the Stuarts save in greater success and greater popularity. Had he been an autocrat, his short reign would seem, from the internal point of view, sadly disappointing, for an autocrat can and should do much. The wonder with Cromwell was that, his resources and powers being so limited, he did anything at all.

At the dissolution of his last Parliament Cromwell was already on the threshold of his sixtieth year. A life of unceasing physical exertion had undermined his health. He had been ill in Ireland and seriously ill in Scotland in 1651. He had been ill in January, 1657, and again at the end of the year. In the meantime his recreations were still of that strenuous kind which had diverted his youth. In his lighter moments he had time to interest himself in agricultural and domestic matters, particularly in the breeding of horses. Once, in the autumn of 1654, when the six Barbary horses which he had been driving in Hyde Park took fright and bolted, he had to jump for his life. Beyond a bruise and a sprain, no serious injury resulted.

Throughout the year 1658 he seemed well enough to the casual observer, but he was already an old man and troubles began to weigh on him. He had never carried them lightly and the prolonged strain of " wrestling with the Lord " over every decision was bound to wear him out in the end. His immense confidence was not of that kind which brings with it a buoyant light-heartedness under responsibility. He knew that he was right, but not without long preliminary struggles ; once even it was alleged that he had striven so hard with the Lord in the privacy of his room that his tears trickled out under the door – a malicious piece of Royalist mockery, but based on the truth that he prayed with a vehemence and physical exertion which prostrated him.

His mother, whose steady devotion had supported him to the very height of his career, died soon after his elevation to power. Her body was laid far away from the quiet land where she had spent her youth and womanhood, far from the bones of her unambitious husband, in the vaults of Westminster Abbey – the first of the Cromwell family to intrude on those exclusive precincts.

At the end of 1657, within a week of each other, Cromwell's " little wenches," Frances and Mary, now nineteen and twenty years old, were married to young Robert Rich, grandson of the Earl of Warwick, and Lord Fauconberg. But Frances was left a widow within three months of her marriage. A far heavier blow to Cromwell was the death in August, 1658, of Elizabeth Claypole, who died horribly and slowly of cancer at the age of twenty-nine. The frivolous little hoyden Betty, with her unashamed Royalism, her sympathetic intervention for the vanquished, and her pretty ways, was by a long way the dearest of his children. It was an open secret that she could manage him when no one else could, although the casual attitude to politics which she shared with her brother Dick prevented her from playing any leading part in Court intrigue. Her frankly unregenerate husband, the jovial Claypole, was in any case a misfit in Protectoral society.

The summer had been marked abroad by the resounding victory in Flanders at the Battle of the Dunes and the cession of Dunkirk to England. It was marked at home by the explosion of one last unsuccessful Royalist conspiracy and by the gathering menace of financial collapse. The treasure taken at Santa Cruz had been used up, the situation in the Navy was critical – Blake's genius at sea had not been paralleled by any administrative genius at home – and the Government's debts were soaring up towards the 2 million mark. Cromwell knew he would have to risk another Parliament and had already made up his mind to call it when his daughter died.

This was on August 16th, 1658. From that day Cromwell's physical resistance crumbled. By the end of the month he had recovered enough from a bad attack of colic and gout to venture out again into the fresh air. It must have been at this time that George Fox met him riding in Hampton Court Park and " saw and felt a waft of death go forth against him : and when I came to him he looked like a dead man."

The Protector was well enough to make his way back to Whitehall to his wife before the last relapse set in. After long hours of restless fever, he died on that same day which had seen his triumphs at Worcester and Dunbar, on September 3rd, at four in the afternoon, while out of the sultry air a torrential thunderstorm burst across the land.

In those last hours he uttered broken words of prayer, noted down and perhaps a little put together by those who waited at his bedside. " Lord," Cromwell had prayed in the intervals of sleep and fever, " Lord . . . I may, I will come

to Thee for Thy people. Thou hast made me,
though very unworthy, a mean instrument to do
them some good, and Thee service : and many
of them have set too high a value upon me. . . .
Lord, however Thou do dispose of me, continue
and go on to do good for them. Give them consistency of judgment, one heart and mutual love :
and go on to deliver them . . . and make the
name of Christ glorious in the world. Teach
those who look too much on Thy instruments to
depend more upon Thyself. Pardon such as
desire to trample upon the dust of a poor worm,
for they are Thy people too."

Rumour ran wild as Cromwell lay dying. Some
said General Lambert would succeed him, as the
best man in the Army and the strongest personality among all those who had fought in the war.
Others were for Fleetwood, Bridget's husband.
A third party suggested that Fairfax, still barely
fifty years old, was to be brought out of retirement.
A fourth and smaller party murmured the name of
young Henry Cromwell. None of these succeeded. Richard Cromwell, at thirty-two, vague,
intelligent, good-natured and weak-minded, had
been nominated by his father : Richard Cromwell
succeeded.

Until the passing of the *Humble Petition and
Advice* Cromwell had made no effort to found a
dynasty, and even afterwards, when by a choice
of successor the way had been thrown open to
him, he had done very little towards it, so little
that one is almost tempted to believe that he did
not himself trust in the permanency of the Protectorate. There was a kind of fatalism about
the choice of Richard. He had the negative
moral virtue that he was not likely to make
trouble, and the negative political advantage that

his succession, unlike that of any of the others,
would not precipitate a split in the country. As
far as the Cromwell family was concerned, it had
no support as such. The Protector had sought no
splendid alliances abroad and had not even
thought out the marriages of his daughters with
any idea of reconciling the dissident groups in
England. The family now stood or fell by its
own merits, and by its own merits it fell – not
unwillingly. After the Restoration Richard
naturally had to go abroad for some time, but,
like all the rest of his family, he eventually died in
England. None of them, not even Henry,
achieved any further distinction save that of being
pointed out in streets and public places as the
children of Oliver Cromwell – with interest and
awe rather than with abhorrence. Bridget, a stern
and hefty old lady, was seen at the Court of
Queen Anne looking, it was said, remarkably like
her father. Frances and Mary continued their
undistinguished and not unhappy lives as ladies
of society, Frances consoling herself for her husband's early death by marrying Sir John Russell.
Their mother lived out her days in the restful
atmosphere of an English country house, never,
one imagines, much regretting the irksome
splendours of Whitehall. She had been there but
five years of a long life, the shortest time that she
and her husband had lived anywhere except at
St. Ives.

Much though not all of Cromwell's work died
with him. His immediate service had been to
stop the civil strife of England and give her back
unity and self-respect. His more permanent service was to strengthen and develop the spirit of
religious enquiry, of individualism and of resistance to mental authority among the English,

which flowered into the ineradicable, indestructible, harsh, fertile, stubborn growth of Nonconformity. His reforms might be swept away by the cross-currents and changes of the Restoration. Fundamentally, the mark he had left on English history stayed for ever.

His body, buried with great pomp in the Abbey, was disinterred two years later and hanged at Tyburn ; the last fate of his bones has never been conclusively proved. They have long since mouldered into the earth of his native land.

Many different estimates of his moral character and his aspirations have been made. In his last years he had often spoken bitterly, calling the people " a many-headed beast, incapable of reason," and declaring that the sword alone was the best argument. Yet, casting up such statements against others of a more generous kind, it is easy to see that even to the end he hoped for some better foundation for his government than mere force. Intensely, tragically he loved the people and felt his responsibility towards them, nor did he ever wholly lose touch with them. To them his last thoughts turned : for them he prayed.

Even that last prayer shows how little he believed in force as a true basis for government. In the twilight of consciousness he uttered the phrase which gives the key to all : " consistency of judgment, one heart and mutual love " – the only foundation for the permanent society. Dying, he could be again the idealist and the Christian that he had been before and, in all those years of stress, had vainly striven still to be.

The old story went on without end, his life but an incident in an unending sequence – force answered by force bringing forth chaos, and

chaos brought to order again by force. His
career resolves itself into a statement of that problem which we to-day are once more called upon
to solve. We need not here discuss the nature of
civil liberty ; it is always a limited and partial
thing, as much in our time as in Cromwell's,
though in different ways. Such as it was, Cromwell believed in it and fought for it. But while
the war lasted liberty was at an end, and when the
wars were over the liberty of the victors became
the oppression of the vanquished. The dominating power in the State changes its name, not its
nature.

Yet against this worst of all disillusionments –
the discovery that the thing saved was not the
thing fought for – Cromwell had his armour.
Even in his moments of deep anxiety he kept that
passionate belief in God which lends to his actions
something at once fantastic and sublime. He never
learnt the politicians's cynicism and he turned his
back deliberately on the obvious truth that in the
affairs of the world there is no right and wrong,
but only the expedient and the inexpedient. He
was spared the humiliation and self-contempt
which, had he had a more acutely logical mind,
he could not have avoided ; for while he acted as
circumstances dictated, he never ceased to believe
that this doubtful compulsion was " none other
than the hand of God."

For many years the term " Regicide " blotted
Cromwell out of the acknowledged ranks of England's heroes. Yet in spite of this his name is
written large on our history. He belongs, like
Queen Elizabeth, to the tradition which has made
this country what it is, and given its people their
reputation, for better, for worse, among their
European fellows. As Elizabeth. with her

commercial acumen, her sense of compromise, her rather simple love of show, was typical of certain aspects of the English character, so too is Cromwell typical with his Juggernaut self-righteousness, his indignation at other people's injustices, his blindness to his own, his sincerity, his lack of intellectual doubt, his fundamental kindness.

His monument has been incongruously set up outside that House of Commons which he so frequently defied. His true monument is neither cast in bronze nor written in books : rather is it to be found in the mark of his personality lying still heavy upon us, in our admirations and our hatreds, our fear and our hope.

BIBLIOGRAPHICAL NOTE
(Revised to 1961)

A full bibliography of Oliver Cromwell was compiled by Professor Wilbur Cortez Abbott (Cambridge, Mass., 1929). I have only attempted here to list a few suggestions for further reading together with some of the more significant books which have appeared since this short biography was first published in 1939.

Carlyle's *Letters and Speeches of Oliver Cromwell* remains the classic treatment of his character. Professor Abbott's *Writings and Speeches of Oliver Cromwell* in four volumes (1937–51) has replaced it for purposes of scholarly study. Among contemporary works which throw light on Cromwell's character Ludlow's *Memoirs* in the edition of Sir Charles Firth is perhaps the most important. *The Journal of George Fox* contains some interesting passages. The poems of Andrew Marvell, written for state occasions during the Protectorate and printed in Margoliouth's edition of Marvell's works, reflect Cromwell's reputation, achievement and personal character at their highest and best.

Of the many biographies of Cromwell that by Sir Charles Firth, published in 1900 and re-issued in The World's Classics with an introduction by G. M. Young in 1953, still holds its own. John Buchan (1934) is especially good on the military side. Maurice Ashley has published three books on Cromwell: *Cromwell, the conservative dictator* (1937), *The Greatness of Oliver Cromwell* (1957) and *Oliver Cromwell and the Puritan Revolution* (1958). In these he has re-assessed Cromwell's character and position in history with thoroughness and sympathy in the light of modern research. A useful analysis of Cromwell's religious thought is to be found in S. Paul, *The Lord Protector: Religion and Politics in the life of Oliver Cromwell* (1955).

S. R. Gardiner, *Cromwell's Place in History* (1897) can be compared with Sir Ernest Barker, *Oliver Cromwell and the English People* (1937), and with Christopher Hill's tercentenary pamphlet written for the Historical Association, *Oliver Cromwell 1658–1958*. In *Charles I and Cromwell* (1936, re-issued 1950) G. M. Young gave a lively picture of the clash of personalities in the critical year 1647.

On the military side Sir Charles Firth, *Cromwell's Army* (third edition 1921) is still indispensable. For Cromwell's lieutenants there is Maurice Ashley *Cromwell's Generals* (1954) and Sir James Berry and Stephen Lee, *A Cromwellian Major General* (1938). For the Civil War see A. J. Burne and Peter Young, *The Great Civil War* (1959), C. V. Wedgwood, *The King's War* (1959) and Austin Woolrych, *Battles of the English Civil War* (1961). The last is outstandingly good on Marston Moor and Preston.

For the Navy, besides Oppenheim's *History of the Administration of the Royal Navy* there is also his article on "The Navy of the Commonwealth" (*English Historical Review*, XI.) from which the quotations on pp. 123 and 125 are taken.

For Ireland massive information is to be found in Prendergast, *The Cromwellian Settlement in Ireland* (second edition, 1922) and in D. Murphy, *Cromwell in Ireland* (1883). Special aspects of Cromwell's rule in England are dealt with by Maurice Ashley, *Financial and Commercial Policy under the Cromwellian Protectorate* (1934) and Menna Prestwich, *Diplomacy and Trade in the Protectorate* (Journal of Modern History, 1950).

For the general history of the period the great work of S. R. Gardiner continued by Sir Charles Firth is still an invaluable guide. So, in a 'more compact form, is Godfrey Davies, *The Early Stuarts* (1937). G. M. Trevelyan, *England under the Stuarts*, first written more than half a century ago, is by now a classic. More recent general histories which incorporate more modern research and give some insight into the present controversial attitude towards the Puritan Revolution are Ashley's volume on the Stuarts in the *Pelican History of England*, and Christopher Hill, *The Century of Revolution* (1961). For the much discussed question of the gentry and the Civil War see Professor H. R. Trevor Roper *The Gentry 1540–1640* (1953) and the answer by Professor R. H. Tawney, " The Rise of the Gentry " (*Economic History Review*, 1954). In *Re-appraisals* (1961) Professor J. H. Hexter has reprinted " Storm over the Gentry ", a trenchant, witty and controversial attack on both sides.

For the thought and atmosphere of the period the most important books are G. N. Clark, *The Seventeenth Century* (second edition, 1947), and Basil Willey, *The Seventeenth Century Background* (1934). For religious and political thought the most vital works are the edition by A. S. P. Woodhouse of the Army debates of 1647, *Puritanism and Liberty* (second edition, 1951) and the two richly informative and fascinating volumes on the Puritans by Professor William Haller, *The Rise of Puritanism* (1938) and *Liberty and Reformation* (1955).